STUDENT SURVIVAL KIT

AN ESSENTIAL GUIDE FOR NEW CHRISTIANS

RALPH W. NEIGHBOUR, JR.

LifeWay Press®
Nashville, Tennessee

© 2007 LifeWay Press®
Reprinted 2008, 2009, 2010, 2011, 2012, 2013
Revised 2016
Reprinted July 2018, Nov. 2018

ISBN: 978-1-4300-6357-5
Item 005791183

Dewey Decimal Classification: 248.4
Subject Heading: CHRISTIAN LIFE \ SALVATION

Printed in the United States of America

Student Ministry Publishing
LifeWay Resources
One LifeWay Plaza
Nashville, TN 37234

We believe that the Bible has God for its author; salvation for its end; and truth, without any
mixture of error, for its matter and that all Scripture is totally true and trustworthy. To review
LifeWay's doctrinal guideline, please visit www.lifeway.com/doctrinalguideline.

CONTENTS

INTRODUCTION

BEGINNING YOUR WALK WITH JESUS CHRIST

You have made life's most important decision. You have given your life to Jesus Christ. Your commitment is based on your faith that He is the Son of God, that He has the power to be your Lord.

This book is called *Student Survival Kit*. It has been written for you by those who have been where you are. Please don't misunderstand the term *survival*. It does not imply that you may lose your relationship to Jesus Christ. You won't ever lose your salvation. In fact, Jesus said: "I give eternal life to them, and they shall never perish; and no one shall snatch them out of My hand" (John 10:28, NASB). Instead, *survival* refers to your ability to function as a new Christian, growing spiritually and living victoriously. The purpose of this book is to help you begin right now to put into action your decision to make Christ your Savior and your Lord.

Certain truths are implied in such a lifetime decision. Your faith in Christ's lordship is based on the fact that:

- Before now you have lived for yourself
- God did not create you to live in such a manner
- God has a greater purpose for your life
- You will find that greater purpose for your life only by making Jesus Christ the Lord of all you are

THINK BACK TO YOUR CONVERSION

Perhaps you thought a great deal about Christ's death on the cross. Your past attempts at trying to do God's job—choosing right and wrong for yourself—may have bothered you. How could you ever face God?

Christ's suffering made it possible for you to be forgiven and to have an open relationship with God.

You prayed, confessing your sin and need for God. You knew God's forgiveness in that moment. You welcomed Christ's control as you turned away from your old values and your old lifestyle. As you prayed, you were reborn! In your physical birth, you were placed in a physical world. In this new, spiritual birth, you were placed in a spiritual world. New values and a new lifestyle awaited you. It was all brand new, wasn't it? The joy, the exhilaration...like suddenly coming from death to life!

NOW

You want to let Jesus be Lord. The problem is, there are so many things you want to know. You are like any new baby: you have life; now you need nourishment to grow. There are many biblical truths you need to feed on right at the start.

FIRST

Set apart a definite time and place to meet your Lord daily. This is a matter of discipline. Without it, you will not grow spiritually as you should. Whether you call it your "quiet time" or "time alone with God," don't delay. Begin now. The time should be as regular as your schedule allows. To help you, the first week of your *Student Survival Kit* will give you practical pointers for a lifetime of quiet times. Also, the whole book is written to provide you with guidance for time alone with God each week. These daily exercises will help you to develop this discipline.

For this reason, resist the temptation to do more than one day's work in this book at a time. Remember: the material has been written to develop new habits in your life. These new patterns of life with Christ in control will take time to develop. As they do, you will feel pulled between your old habits and your new ones. This is normal. All of us have experienced it. Old patterns of thinking and acting will be clashing constantly with new ones. Old habits will be confronted with the demands of Christ. Your daily quiet time will become the first new discipline of your Christian life.

You will continually learn new truths about your faith, but five are critical for your immediate survival. You will become acquainted with them next.

WHAT'S IN YOUR SURVIVAL KIT?

The contents of your survival kit can be put on the fingers of one hand. Your hand can help you remember the five truths you will be learning. The illustration at the right identifies these five truths. The thumb works in cooperation with each finger. The first truth you will learn has a working relationship with each of the other four. You always must combine the first truth with the rest to survive as a Christian.

The materials you will study are designed to help you understand how God works in your life and in your world. In addition, when you have finished, you will be able to explain to your non-Christian friends many important facts about your new faith.

You face many problems and temptations daily. Your survival kit has been written to guide you through the common struggles faced by most new believers. Keep in mind, though, that what you will learn is only a foundation (like a building's foundation) for your new life. A great number of floors will be built upon it in the years to come as you grow in Bible understanding, develop discipleship skills, and learn to participate in the missions outreach of your church. This will happen as you participate actively in studying God's Word, training, worship, and missions opportunities in your church. However, these opportunities are not an end in themselves. They do not guarantee spiritual growth. Instead, they provide a chance for you to encounter God, to hear from Him, to respond to Him, and to grow in your relationship with Him.

MOST NEW CHRISTIANS GO THROUGH THESE STAGES

1. The Excitement Stage

As a new Christian, you are aware that Jesus Christ has literally come to live in your life. The life you now live is new! Naturally, you will want to share this new life with your unbelieving friends. This is a happy stage!

THE FIVE TRUTHS OF THE CHRISTIAN FAITH

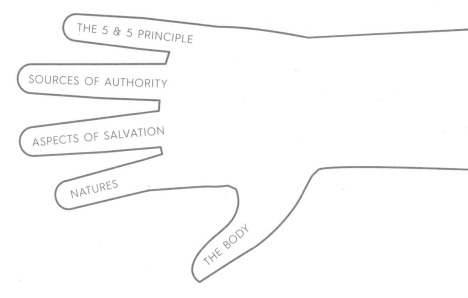

THE 5 & 5 PRINCIPLE

SOURCES OF AUTHORITY

ASPECTS OF SALVATION

NATURES

THE BODY

During this excitement stage, the most important fact for you to learn is that you are now a part of the body of Christ, the church—a local group of fellow believers. Placing you in that body is one of the first works of the Holy Spirit. Being baptized in water is your public witness to that fact. Baptism tells the whole world that you have become new and that your life now belongs to the Lord Jesus Christ.

If you think only about your own personal relationship to Christ, you will miss a great truth:

Your Christian growth depends strongly on your relationship to the body of Christ, the church.

2. The Fight Stage

Perhaps you have boasted to a few of your unbelieving friends of your new victory over temptation. It is true that such a victory is real in your life, but things are not always smooth. Tempers flare. Frustrations return. Resentment creeps in... along with jealousy, criticism, and gossip. You discover that these old habits and temptations still bother you.

Now you face the danger of acting the part of a victorious Christian. You think, *I'll just cover this up. No one ever has to know that I'm really struggling. I'll look bad if I admit I still fight temptation.* You become busy at church, thinking that going to every church event will help. After a while you can no longer fool yourself; you have started to live a lie. You have no inner victory. You are defeated. You feel like a hypocrite. You have become a defeated Christian.

Before that happens—before the fight stage begins—you must be introduced to an important truth: When the new nature of Christ entered your life, the old nature did not die. You now possess two natures, not one.

3. The Doubting Stage

If not taught properly, many new Christians will enter a doubting stage. They wrongly think that their salvation is a finished thing, completed the moment they received Christ. In one sense, this is absolutely true:

> *All Christ has to give you was provided in that moment when you became a Christian.*

But it's like receiving a new computer or cell phone as a gift. It's complete when it comes to you, but you must understand it to get the greatest benefit from it. It will take time for you learn the software and unique features.

Jesus promised that when you became a Christian, the Holy Spirit would enter you as a teacher and would teach you all things (John 14:26). As the inner war between the new nature and the old nature takes place, you begin to feel a need for more information about your salvation. You need more truth! You must learn that your salvation has three aspects: it is *a point in time* when Christ enters; *a process of time*, as the power of the new nature gives you victory over sin and the old nature; and *a final point in time*, when Christ will set you free forever from the old nature.

4. The Panic-Search-for-Truth Stage
To spare you from this stage, you will study the source of Christian truth and compare it to three other sources. If you were to ask someone about where truth can be found, one person you talk to may suggest that you use reason or logic to figure out the questions about your new faith. Another may suggest that you rely on a special encounter with God to answer your questions. Still another friend may recommend the traditions of the church and suggest they hold the solutions to your questions.

The first person builds faith on intellect; the second person, on experience; and the third person rests all beliefs on tradition. You will learn that although all three of these sources of authority have a certain place, the true source of authority for a Christian is the written Word of God, the Bible.

5. The "Silent Christian" Stage
Have you already met some "silent Christians" who never witness? If you haven't, you will! You may wonder why they are that way. Perhaps these insights will help you understand them:

1. They feel that other Christians who know more and doubt less should be the ones to share their faith or take a stand.
2. Because they have not "perfected" the Christian life, they do not want to present a bad example or give a false impression of what it means to be a believer.
3. They are uncomfortable with sharing their faith, so they work hard in church activities that do not require any verbal witness to others.

Many Christians sleep in this "Silent Christian" stage! Christians who do not share their faith verbally may be busy in the church, but many allow their questions and fears to keep them from talking with others about what it means to be a believer. Before that happens to you, resolve to study the final section of this book. Learn about the 5 & 5 Principle.

ON THE JOURNEY

This chart shows how the 11-week devotional plan of the Student Survival Kit will prepare you for the various stages of Christian growth. Write in the dates you will begin each five-day quiet time. Begin on Monday. Use Saturday and Sunday to grow with your small group and look back at what God has shown you throughout the week. Check the box at the left after you have completed each week's study.

✓	WEEK	DATE	SUBJECT	STAGE
☐	Week 1		The Indwelling Christ	Excitement
☐	Week 2		One Body *Its Life*	Excitement
☐	Week 3		One Body *Its Service*	Excitement
☐	Week 4		Two Natures *The New Nature*	Fight
☐	Week 5		Two Natures *The Old Nature*	Fight
☐	Week 6		Salvation *Its Beginning & Completion*	Doubting
☐	Week 7		Salvation *A Daily Process*	Doubting
☐	Week 8		Authority *Three Inadequate Sources*	Panic-Search for-Truth
☐	Week 9		Authority *One True Source*	Panic-Search for-Truth
☐	Week 10		The 5 & 5 Principle *In Prayer*	"Silent Christian"
☐	Week 11		The 5 & 5 Principle *In Witnessing*	"Silent Christian"

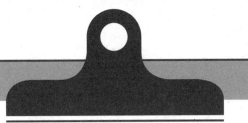

SCRIPTURE MEMORY VERSES

Check the box when you have memorized the Scripture for the week.

Week 1 ☐ **Psalm 119:11**

Week 2 ☐ **Romans 12:4-5**

Week 3 ☐ **1 Peter 4:10**

Week 4 ☐ **Galatians 5:22-23**

Week 5 ☐ **Colossians 3:8-10**

Week 6 ☐ **Philippians 1:6**

Week 7 ☐ **Romans 5:10**

Week 8 ☐ **1 Corinthians 2:14**

Week 9 ☐ **2 Timothy 3:16**

Week 10 ☐ **Philippians 4:6**

Week 11 ☐ **Matthew 28:18-20**

THE INDWELLING CHRIST

I have treasured Your word in my heart so that I may not sin against You. —PSALM 119:11

How to Establish a Quiet Time

Would you expect to be healthy if the only time you ate a meal was on Sunday morning? Of course not! You wouldn't survive long. Do you think you will be any healthier spiritually if you wait until Sunday morning to digest spiritual truth?

A daily quiet time or time of personal worship provides regular contact with your source of spiritual life, Jesus Christ. Each day, you need to find a time to be alone with Christ. Here are some suggestions.

1. *Find a specific time and place*—A desk, a table, or even the side of your bed will do. It is important to schedule at least 10 minutes for your quiet time. If possible, schedule your time with God at the start of your day.

2. *Be consistent*—A hit-and-miss pattern is an indication that you are not as serious as you need to be about growing as a Christian. Your quiet time is when you "program" your day to let Christ be Lord of your life.

3. *Have God's Word and a way to take notes*—For the first 11 weeks of your quiet time, you will be using the *Survival Kit* five days a week. Use your Bible study lesson and take time to look back over what your read during the week on the other two days. You'll want to use a notebook, your phone, or a computer to keep a spiritual growth journal.

4. *Begin with prayer*—Open your heart to Christ, offering Him the right to teach, discipline, or direct you as you study. Tell Him you love Him. Share your concerns with Him.

5. *End with a definite project for the day, related to what you have learned*—Before you end your time alone with God, decide how you can live out the truth you have learned in your quiet time.

HAVE TODAY'S QUIET TIME RIGHT NOW.

Pray. Express your love for God. Thank Him for giving you His life through Christ. Share with Him the special ways you need His power in your life. Ask Him to live through you as you live your life today.

This is how we know that we remain in Him and He in us: He has given assurance to us from His Spirit. And we have seen and we testify that the Father has sent His Son as the world's Savior. Whoever confesses that Jesus is the Son of God— God remains in him and he in God. —1 JOHN 4:13-15

As you read the Bible, God's Word, you are getting spiritual nourishment. But are you "digesting" what you read? One way to help you digest the thoughts in Scripture verses is to rewrite them in your own words. Try doing this now with the verses you have just read. Rewrite them below in your own words:

According to these verses, what gift confirms that you have become a Christian?

As a Christian you have received God's gift of His Holy Spirit. What confession causes God to abide in you and you to abide in God?

As a Christian you have experienced personally that God the Father has sent Jesus Christ to be the Savior—your own Savior, as well as the Savior of the world. In what ways can you live out the truths of 1 John 4:13-15 in today's tasks? What differences will there be in your attitudes? In your actions?

End today's quiet time by writing at least one specific way you will try to put the truths of 1 John 4:13-15 to work in your life today.

DAY 2

Using Your Bible As a Source of Christian Growth

Read Psalms 119:11; 40:8. Memorize Psalm 119:11. Each day you will be given a few Bible verses to study. Your daily quiet time should always focus on Scripture. The indwelling Christ will speak to your heart as you read the Word of God.

Do you have a good study Bible? All Bibles in the English language are called translations because they have been translated from their original languages into English. The original books of the Bible were mainly written in ancient Hebrew and Greek. Because the King James Version was first published in the early 1600s, its wording is often hard for us to understand today. Almost every translation is available on apps for your phone. Try to find at least one of these Bible translations in print or on your phone:

- Holman Christian Standard Bible (HCSB)
- New American Standard Bible (NASB)
- New International Version (NIV)
- New Living Translation (NLT)

If you did not grow up attending church, you may have a problem finding books, chapters, and verses in the Bible. Using the index in the front of your Bible, you will soon learn where they are.

All of today's verses are in Psalms; you will find Psalms exactly in the middle of your Bible. Find and read Psalm 119:11. Where did the writer keep the Word of God?

One way we say "I memorized it" is "I learned it by heart." The writer of Psalm 119:11 used that same word *heart* in saying where he kept God's Word.

The last part of that verse tells one great value of memorizing Scripture. What is that value?

Memorizing God's Word can help you keep from sinning against God. Read Psalm 40:8. If you don't have a Bible in your hand, how can you use your phone or other resources to keep a supply of Scripture close?

No other advice in this book will have greater value for your growth as a Christian than this one: *memorize Scripture on a regular schedule!* To help you get started, 12 verses are printed at the end of your book. Cut them into pocket-sized cards. You can also download scripture memory apps to help you memorize God's Word. The first verse to learn is Psalm 119:11. Memorize one verse each week.

Why bother to learn the exact words of a Scripture verse? Because it is actually easier to recall a verse word for word. It is easier to meditate on a verse when you can repeat it again and again in your mind. Memorized verses give you assurance as a Christian—in fighting temptations to sin, in telling others about Christ, in explaining what you believe. And God wants you to know His Holy Word.

Begin now! Carry the verses with you. Start learning one verse on Monday of each week. Write the verses and display them in places see every day—on the bathroom mirror, on your desk, near the computer. You'll find that disciplining your mind can make use of the time you waste each day. You can memorize while riding, walking, waiting, or resting. Reviewing daily all verses will reinforce them in your memory.

Learn your verses as though your spiritual growth depended on it because it does!

DAY 3

Learning to Pray

Read Matthew 6:9-13. Quote from memory Psalm 119:11. Do you like to talk with your closest friends? Of course! You will also like to talk with your Lord. You don't need to say words like "Thee" and "Thou." God knows the words you normally use. He wants you to speak to Him as a child would speak to a father. Share with Him your feelings, your attitudes, your fears, your desires, and your frustrations. He will understand. He will respond to your prayers.

Jesus' first followers asked Him to teach them to pray. In response He gave them a Model Prayer, which is often called the Lord's Prayer. You can find this Model Prayer in Matthew 6:9-13. Look up Matthew in the index of your Bible. Or try opening your Bible one-fourth of the way from the back. Either way, you'll find Matthew at the beginning of the New Testament, the second big section of your Bible.

Read Matthew 6:9-13 carefully. Copy the Model Prayer on the blank lines below. Begin with "Our Father." Match each phrase or sentence to one part of the outline on the left.

TOPICS IN THE MODEL PRAYER	THE MODEL PRAYER
Addressing God Properly *(v. 9)*	
Showing Respect for God's Name *(v. 9)*	
Committing Ourselves and All on Earth to God's Plans *(v. 10)*	
Asking God to Provide for Our Needs, Not Our Wants *(v. 11)*	
Asking God for Forgiveness *(v. 2)*	
Asking God for Protection *(v. 13)*	
Declaring God's Rule Over Us to Be Our Greatest Wish *(v. 13)*	
Ending Our Prayer Properly *(v. 13)*	

Now use the outline of Jesus' Model Prayer and express your own prayer.

DAY 4
Understanding What Has Happened to You

Read 2 Corinthians 5:17; Colossians 1:27. As you develop your quiet time day by day, you will become aware that some basic changes are happening in your life.

Find and read 2 Corinthians 5:17. As you read 2 Corinthians 5:17, you will realize what has happened in your life. Three key words sum things up. Write them in the proper places below.

Your _____ life is passing away.
Your _____ life is coming into being.
All of these changes are made by _____.

Yes, Christ makes the difference between your old and your new life. You are being changed. You are being made different from other people who do not know Jesus Christ. You are being made different from what you were before you gave your life to Him.

Now look at Colossians 1:27. The last part of that verse tells who is changing your life from old to new. According to Colossians 1:27, where is Christ right now?

Do those two simple little words "in you" remind you of a diagram you have seen in this *Survival Kit*? Do you remember seeing a hand with its fingers? (Hint: look at page 7.)

Write "in you" on the palm in the diagram.

Christ is "in you." He is the indwelling Christ, controlling all. Because of this, your life is changing day by day. Habits are hard to break. As His Holy Spirit within your life takes the fun and joy out of your old, sinful actions, do not let them continue. In prayer, lay them before God and ask Him to remove them.

List some old habits or actions that have already become flat and tasteless to you.

_____ _____

_____ _____

Never forget that Jesus was willing to die for you! Thank Him for that in your daily quiet time. Ask Him to keep on taking away your old habits.

DAY 5

A Basic Principle to Choose By

Read 1 Corinthians 10:31. Quote from memory Psalm 119:11. The Christian faith does not have a long list of do's and don'ts for you to live by. (Beware of those who try to give you one!) Instead, there is a simple principle to choose.

Find and read 1 Corinthians 10:31; then state the principle here.

WHATEVER YOU _ _, _ _ IT _ _ _
FOR THE G _ _ _ _ OF G _ _.

Paul, the writer of 1 Corinthians, made these points very clear:
- Our conduct is a statement of the life we now have in Christ.
- All we do should bring glory to God.

Now apply the basic principle you have just learned: A new Christian was faced with a choice. His best friend, with whom he had smoked marijuana many times, offered him some. He feared that if he refused, his friend would reject him. He desired very much to continue the relationship, hoping he might be able to share Christ with his friend later.

What should the new Christian do? Circle your answer.

   A. **Take one small puff and then decline to take any more.**
   B. **Scold the friend for smoking marijuana.**
   C. **Avoid the issue by making some sort of excuse.**
   D. **Decline, explaining that he had rather not, that since he has become a Christian, Christ has been taking away his desire to smoke marijuana.**

I hope you circled the last suggestion. This alone would bring the greatest glory to God, wouldn't it?

   You will be faced with choices like this constantly. You don't need to act like a self-righteous fanatic. In a loving and gentle spirit, communicate that you are taking a stand for your own conduct. People will respect you for that spirit.

   You have already learned how the Word of God can help you choose between right and wrong. Your Scripture memory verse should remind you of that fact every time you repeat it. **Write Psalm 119:11 in the margin.**

   The verses printed at the end of your *Student Survival Kit* are quoted from the Holman Christian Standard Bible. Maybe you'd rather memorize them from another translation. If so, feel free! Maybe you'd like to write your own Scripture memory cards. Writing the verses word for word, in whatever translation you prefer, is another good way to help you learn them more quickly.

   The following weeks of this *Student Survival Kit* will not tell you day-by-day to have a quiet time. You have already discovered for yourself how much a daily quiet time can strengthen your spiritual growth as a new Christian. Don't forget to pray as you meditate on God's Word. A daily time for prayer and Bible study can be one of the best ways the indwelling Christ makes His presence felt as He controls your life!

ONE BODY
ITS LIFE

WEEK TWO

Now as we have many parts in one body, and all the parts do not have the same function, in the same way we who are many are one body in Christ and individually members of one another. —ROMANS 12:4-5

DAY 1

One Body

Read Romans 12:4-5. Memorize the verses. There is no such thing as "Lone wolf" Christians in God's family! The act of becoming a follower of Jesus Christ is also a commitment to others who have already vowed to follow Him forever.

We can imagine having a family even if a baby isn't born into it. It's possible because of adoption or foster care, but can you imagine a baby surviving without someone to love and to care for it? Of course not! Babies do not survive if left alone. They need constant love, care, and attention. To survive, they must be surrounded by a family—people who are concerned about their survival. Apart from the family of God, you will not grow much spiritually. That family is called by several names: the church, the called-out ones, the body of Christ, the living stones (You will learn more about these names later).

Open your Bible to Romans 12:4-5. These verses state one central truth about the family of God, the church. That truth can be formulated almost like an equation.

Fill in the missing letters, based on what you read in Romans 12:4-5.

M_ _ Y   M_ _ B_ _ _   (or parts) = ONE   _ _ D_

A central truth about the church is its unity. Scripture says, "We are one body in Christ." So you should have written the equation like this:

Many Members (or parts) = One Body

Romans 12:4-5 are the verses you are to memorize this week. Here it is, quoted from the New American Standard Bible (Look up that translation

online or on your app if your don't have it in print). **See if you can
already complete it by filling in four key words, each of which is used
twice in the verse.**

For just as we have _____ _____
in _____ _____ *and all the* _____
*do not have the same function, so we, who
are* _____ *, are* _____ _____ *in
Christ... —ROMANS 12:4-5, NASB*

You should have completed the verse like this: "For just as we have
many members in one body and all the members do not have the same
function, so we, who are many, are one body in Christ."

If you are going to have healthy spiritual growth, you need to be
connected to a church. You will find among church members the love,
nurturing, and care that permit growth to take place. If you have not yet
professed Christ publicly and been baptized into the membership of a
church, you should do so at once. Church membership is not an option or
something to be delayed; *it is the first step to survival as a growing Christian.*

DAY 2

The Church, a Body

Read 2 Timothy 1:8-10; Ephesians 4:1-4. Do you know the meaning
of the word *church*? It is a translation of a Greek word in one of the
original languages of the Bible: *ekklesia (ek-klay-see-ah),* meaning
"called-out ones."

Visualize a large group of people who live by their own personal
desires. Christ calls out to this large group and says, "Follow Me!
Separate yourselves from others who live by their personal desires.
Be My disciples!" Some hear Him... and then turn away. Others make a
clear decision. They come to Christ. They have decided to follow Him.
These are the "called-out ones." They are the church.

You will see the words "called" and "calling" in the Bible passages listed for your reading today.

Look at 2 Timothy 1:8-10. Find in those verses the answers to these questions. Who calls us out?

God calls us out "in Christ Jesus." The character of the called-out ones is described in Ephesians 4:1-4. Find and read those verses now. The power Christ gives lets us live a new lifestyle.

List below some of the characteristics of this new lifestyle made possible by Christ:

_____   _____

_____   _____

_____   _____

_____   _____

The lifestyle pictured in Ephesians 4:1-4 is clear. Humility, gentleness, patience, endurance, love—these characteristics will show in the lives of Christ's called-out ones.

Which characteristic would you most desire for others to see in your life today? Mark your initials beside it in the list.

Here is a deep thought: Christ will not give you that characteristic. You see, He is that characteristic. Christ is humble, gentle, patient, loving, and all the rest. You must let Christ be Lord, and He will reveal to those you meet this day that part of His nature which now lives in you!

Did you notice a familiar two-word phrase in Ephesians 4:4? Note that the called-out ones are referred to in that verse as "one body." Tomorrow you will continue thinking about this important idea.

DAY 3

No Divisions in the Body

Read 1 Corinthians 12:14-27. Quote from memory Romans 12:4-5.
Perhaps you have already discovered that Jesus often taught His followers using stories. Books of the Bible written by the apostle Paul contain few stories, but your Bible reading for today sounds like one of the parables told by Jesus. In this case, Paul was doing the storytelling.

In 1 Corinthians 12:14-27 Paul compared Christ's called-out ones to parts of a human body. Each part is unique but connected to the rest. Christ is equally present in the hand, in the foot, or in an inner organ. All are interdependent; no member can survive without help from other members. What a powerful description of life in the body of Christ!

Your growth in the Christian life is related directly to those you are related to in the body of Christ. When one suffers, all hurt. When one rejoices, all are happy. That's why baptism and the Lord's Supper are celebrated when all the members of the church are together. For example, all the members celebrate when you, by your baptism, give witness to your new life in Christ. In the Lord's Supper, all the members share symbolically the life provided by the death of Christ. These are events in the life of the body of Christ. They cannot be enjoyed by those who are not a part of the body.

How much do you know about baptism and the Lord's Supper? Stop now and test your knowledge.

Mark *B* for baptism or *LS* for Lord's Supper beside each of the statements listed below:
____1. Described in 1 Corinthians 11:23-26.
____2. Described in Romans 6:4.
____3. Experienced personally by a Christian one time only.
____4. Experienced personally by a Christian many times.
____5. Symbolizes Jesus' broken body and shed blood.
____6. Symbolizes Jesus' death and resurrection.
____7. Symbolizes a Christian's death to sin and new life in Christ.
____8. Commanded to be done by all who follow Christ.
____9. Usually described as one of the two ordinances of the church.

Answers: 1—LS; 2—B; 3—B; 4—LS; 5—LS; 6—B; 7—B; 8—either or both; 9—either.

DAY 4

The Church, a Building

Read 1 Peter 2:1-10; Ephesians 2:19-22. You are learning two Bible verses that speak of that "one body," made up of all who follow Christ. Fill in the key words "one," "body," and "members" at the proper places in the verses. (Hint: Look back at yesterday's work!)

*Now as we have many _____ in _____ _____,
and all _____ the same function,
in the same way we who are many
are _____ _____ in Christ and individually
members of one another. —ROMANS 12:4-5*

In 1 Peter 2:1-10 and Ephesians 2:19-22, the called-out ones are described as a building rather than as a body. Christ is "the head of the body, the church" (Col. 1:18). But He is also the "precious corner stone" of the building (1 Pet. 2:6). We are described as "living stones." We are being constructed into a "spiritual house," a "holy temple."

When builders build a wall from stones, they must chip away on each one, smoothing and shaping it. Soon it has the proper form to be fitted against the stones around it. This shows why you must be a part of a church to grow properly. *God's shaping process in your life requires you to be related properly to other living stones.* He chips away at your character until you are bonded together with the other living stones.

Some stones have rough edges. **Read 1 Peter 2:1. What are some of the "rough edges" God may chip away from your life?**

Actually, two kinds of stones are mentioned in 1 Peter 2:1-10. You and I and all other Christians are like stones with rough edges—envy, hypocrisy, and all the other evils listed in verse 1. But Jesus Christ, our sinless Lord and Savior, is the "choice" or "precious" or "valuable" cornerstone described in verse 6.

Now look again at Ephesians 2:19-22. What "cement" bonds together the living stones that make up the church?

Christ Jesus Himself joins us with one another in His church. According to verse 22, what is the only purpose for the existence of this building made up of believers?

Isn't it great to know that you and your fellow believers help to form a building in which God's Holy Spirit lives? Are you beginning to realize that you, as an individual member of the body (or the "building") of believers, truly need the others God has called out?

List below two areas in your life as a Christian that you know will not develop correctly apart from other believers.

Whatever you wrote, be sure to pray about it when you have your daily quiet time. Ask God to help you grow in relationship with your fellow believers. Also, don't forget to review the verses you have been memorizing.

Place a check beside the reference of each verse that you can repeat aloud from memory right now.

_____ Psalm 119:11   _____ Romans 12:4-5

DAY 5

New Life in the Body

Read Acts 2:42-47; 4:32-35. Quote from memory Psalm 119:11 and Romans 12:4-5. These passages can be difficult for twenty-first century Christians to understand until we discover the true meaning of the church for ourselves. From time to time, Christians sold a portion of their belongings and shared it through the apostles as others in the body (church) had need. Those who had more than they needed shared with other people. As they did, they were confident that God would, in turn, supply all their needs.

They shared far more than money. They shared whole lives with one another—eating, praying, sharing in Bible study, and teaching. Their lifestyle showed that they had been called out from other people. The life of the called-out ones was not marked by the closed, selfish spirit found among unbelievers. Instead, they had a unique family life together.

The fellowship you share with other believers is a vital part of your growth in Christ. Plunge deeply into the family of God and develop relationships with those who are your new brothers and sisters in the family.

Now let's compare Acts 2:42-45 and Acts 4:32-35. Both of these passages describe three important aspects of the church—then and now.

Read the verses marked on the first two columns of the chart. Then try to complete the summary sentence. Do the same thing with the second and third lines.

ACTS 2	ACTS 4	LIFE IN THE CHURCH
44	32	Church members are _____ in Christ.
45	34-35	Church members should _____ their lives.
42-43	33	Church members should _____ their Lord.

It probably wasn't hard to remember that church members are one body in Christ. And a little while ago you read that church members should share their lives. What did you write on the third line? "Proclaim"? "Witness for"? "Tell people about"? Any of those would be correct.

Read Acts 2:45 again. Which would be more difficult for you: to sell a personal possession to help a needy member of the church body or to be on the receiving end of such a gift? Why?

Now write below Romans 12:4-5. *(This is one of your memory passages.)*

ONE BODY
ITS SERVICE

Based on the gift each one has received, use it to serve others, as good managers of the varied grace of God. –1 PETER 4:10

DAY 1

One Body to Reflect God's Love

Read 1 Corinthians 13:1-13. **Memorize 1 Peter 4:10.** You have read one of the most beautiful chapters in the Bible. It is also one of the most famous passages in world literature.

What is the greatest thing in the world, according to the verses that you read today?

If you read 1 Corinthians 13 in the King James Version, you may have written the word *charity* on that blank line. Almost all other translations of the Bible use *love*. Love is the greatest thing in the world! God is that love, and Christ's love in you flows to others. *The body of Christ is made to reveal love!* Unbelievers are changed by the love of Christ.

Now take a closer look at 1 Corinthians 13. In verses 1-3, which of these qualities are described as being inferior to love? (Check the boxes.)

☐ **Great spiritual knowledge**   ☐ **Mighty faith**

☐ **Generosity to the poor**   ☐ **Being willing to die for truth**

☐ **Powers of speaking**   ☐ **All of these qualities**

Did you realize that all of these qualities are mentioned in 1 Corinthians 13:1-3? Maybe you checked that last box; or maybe you just checked each of the other boxes individually. Remember: The point Paul, the writer of 1 Corinthians, made was that all of these qualities, good and even great as they may be, are not as great as love.

All of these qualities are yours as a Christian. God is love. And the Son of God, the indwelling Christ, will make these qualities of love more and more apparent in your life as you let Him live in you.

Paul used two figures of speech in 1 Corinthians 13:11-12. List in the space below these two analogies:

Verse 12 describes our limited human knowledge as dim shadows seen in a mirror. Verse 11 compares it to babbling like a child. That's why knowledge is not as great as love.

When God added you to His body, He made you a working member of it. He provided you with spiritual "gifts." Think of the gifts of the Spirit as riverbeds through which Christ's love flows. The faster a river flows, the deeper the riverbed is cut. As God's love flows through you, your gifts deepen. Their purpose is to let more of Christ's love flow to others! You are to be a channel for His love. That is why He has given you gifts.

This truth is made plain in the verse you should be memorizing during the week, 1 Peter 4:10. Write it here.

DAY 2
Every Member Has a Function

Read 1 Corinthians 12:4-7. Every member of the body of Christ has a function. God added you to the body to be a working member of it. When He did so, He gave you special abilities called gifts. Two of these gifts are basic to all the other gifts. They are the gift of service and the gift of giving. You should be using these two gifts today. As you are obedient to Christ, the Head of the body, He will deepen your channel of love—your riverbed. Other gifts will mature in you. Many require a deeper level of maturity to be exercised.

There is a difference between gifts and talents. A gift is a spiritual power possessed only by Christians. On the other hand, both Christians and non-Christians possess talents. For example, piano playing is a talent. Faith is a gift and is used to glorify God.

List some of the talents you possess that you can use to glorify God rather than only to bring glory to yourself.

Keep memorizing 1 Peter 4:10. Now look at another part of the Bible that also tells about gifts. Read 1 Corinthians 12:4-6. In whatever translation you are using, it should be clear that each of these three short verses shows a contrast. Summarize those three contrasts by completing this simple chart.

1 CORINTHIANS 12	DIFFERENT	THE SAME
Verse 4	Gifts	Spirit
Verse 5		
Verse 6		

All the words you have written in the "*Different*" column of the chart should have something to do with gifts and how they're used. All the words you have written in "*The Same*" column of the chart should be names for the One who gives you these gifts. **Why does God give you these gifts through His Spirit?**

The purpose is stated in 1 Corinthians 12:7. Read that verse; then place a check mark beside the right answer.

☐ **For the good of the person receiving the gift**
☐ **For the good of all (the common good)**

You should have checked the second of the two answers.

DAY 3

Obedience

Read Romans 12:1-8. Quote from memory 1 Peter 4:10. Would you trust a thousand dollars to the care of a servant who did not obey your commands? Of course not!

God has provided you with many spiritual gifts. Before they will become available for your use, however, you must first prove yourself obedient to Christ, the Head of the body. **Look now at the title for Day 3.** The key to the gifts God gives you is obedience. God gives gifts to those He can trust to obey Him.

Read Romans 12:1-3 to help you realize what obedience requires.

Here are five key words or phrases from those verses.

Transformed

Conformed

Sacrifice

Think Highly

Will of God

In Romans 12:1-3, two of these five key words or phrases are used to state what you cannot do if you are obedient to your Lord. The other three are used to state what you must do.

Try now to write those five statements briefly, using the key words and phrases from Romans 12:1-3.

What you cannot do:

What you must do:

Now check what you have written by this example. Your statements may vary somewhat, according to which version you are using.

What you must not do: *Be conformed to this world.*
Think too highly of yourself.

What you must do: *Give yourself as a living sacrifice.*
Be transformed (by the indwelling Christ).
Do the will of God.

Do you struggle with the thought that you're called to be obedient to Christ? If so, can you list some reasons for your struggle?

What parts of being called to be obedient challenge what you valued before knowing Christ?

DAY 4

The Gift of Service

Read 1 Corinthians 1:4-8; 16:15-16. Your next reading includes a few verses from the first chapter of 1 Corinthians, plus a few verses from the last chapter.

Check the reference of the passage that mentions the gift of service.

☐ **1 Corinthians 1:4-8**
☐ **1 Corinthians 16:15-16**

The gift of service, mentioned in 1 Corinthians 16:15-16, is sometimes called the gift of administration. The word literally describes someone who serves as a waiter at a dinner table. It is used to mean any activity of service motivated by the love of Christ within us.

Serving the Lord in the simple things is an expression of obedience. Christ was willing to wash the feet of His disciples. It was not beneath His dignity. That same Christ is now Lord of your life. If you are not faithful to Him in small things, should you expect Him to give you greater ministries to perform?

Read 1 Corinthians 1:4-8 again. From these verses, do you get the assurance that you have immediate use of some gifts upon giving your life to Christ as Lord and Savior? Why or why not?

Read 1 Corinthians 16:15-16. These verses mention that Stephanas' family was performing a task. What words does your translation use to describe the task?

Actually, 1 Corinthians 16:15 says in the original language that this family of Christians devoted themselves to using the gift of service. Whom were they serving?

The word *saints* in 1 Corinthians 16:15 means Christians, the called-out ones, not people who are considered "super Christians" or people whose names are on a special list.

Look at 1 Corinthians 16:16. How are we to treat fellow members of the body of Christ who exercise the gift of service?

We are to follow the leadership of those who exercise the gift of service; we are to submit or subject ourselves to them.

You possess the gift of service! We may all serve others in different ways, but you have it nonetheless. Christ's presence within your life will express itself first by teaching you the great value of serving others. It is the basic gift for all ministries to follow, for all years to come. You can begin to exercise it today.

Pray about the answer to this question: In *what ways are believers called to serve others in the body of Christ today?*

Now let's do a little checking. How are you surviving as a new Christian? Remember, you have Christ's promise in John 10:28 that you will never lose your relationship to Him as Lord and Savior. But it's still good to check up on yourself now and then. Being held accountable for your daily walk with Christ is part of being a believer.

It's been nearly three weeks since you began using your *Student Survival Kit*. How many days in those three weeks have you had a quiet time, including prayer and Bible study? Circle the number of days.

1 2 3 4 5 6 7 8 9 10 11 12 13 14 15 16 17 18 19 20

How many Scripture verses have you committed to memory? Circle the references for the ones you can repeat aloud right now. If you're struggling with remembering them, take a few minutes and review them right now.

Psalm 119:11   **Romans 12:4-5**   **1 Peter 4:10**

DAY 5
The Gift of Giving

Read 2 Corinthians 8:1-5; 9:6-15. Quote from memory Psalm 19:11; Romans 12:4-5; and 1 Peter 4:10.

"Giving" describes *someone deliberately parting with their things so that a change of ownership is brought about.* Such giving is the result of the Holy Spirit's work. When you recognize that Jesus Christ is the owner of all you possess, it isn't hard to share! You will have problems only when you continue to consider possessions as yours. The key is letting the Spirit lead you to give what you have in ministering to others. You do this by firmly believing that God will supply your needs continually and that God is perfectly able to replenish your supply. After all, when God causes you to give to others, you can trust Him completely to care for your own needs.

Read 2 Corinthians 8:1-5. List the words used to describe Christians. Do you think the believers described in these verses could really afford to give so much? Why or why not?

Did you write words like "poor," "poverty," "trouble," or "affliction"? Members of the churches in Macedonia were not rich, yet they gave.

Read 2 Corinthians 9:6-15. Among verses 6-10, which two verses give strongest assurance that God will supply the source of your giving?

Verse _____ and verse _____.

Verses 8 and 10 give this assurance. **In verse 11, what is the ultimate purpose for your being enriched?**

Your generous giving to others is made possible by God's generous giving to you. It results in others praising God. When you give to others, they are drawn to him.

According to 2 Corinthians 9:13, how does the watching world respond to Christians giving to help one another? Who gets the greatest benefit when you give?

Often, people see God because Christians give to help one another.

What specific commitment is Christ calling you to make as you begin to exercise this basic gift of giving? *(Remember: He is more interested in whether your giving is an act of obedience than He is in how much you give.)*

TWO NATURES, PART ONE
THE NEW NATURE

But the fruit of the Spirit is love, joy, peace, patience, kindness, goodness, faith, gentleness, self-control. Against such things there is no law. —GALATIANS 5:22-23

DAY 1

The New Nature

Read Galatians 5:13-18. Memorize Galatians 5:22-23. Did you know that you now have two natures instead of one? Since birth, you have had an old sinful nature. After your spiritual birth, you have had a new nature. The old nature seeks to exalt self; the new nature seeks to allow the love of God to flow through you.

Now see what the Scriptures say about your two natures. **Find and read Galatians 5:13-18.** In verses 13-14 you will note a key word used twice. This word tells how your new nature functions in your life as a Christian.

What is that key word?

One way your new nature functions in love is through giving. Yes, your new nature functions in love. But not your old nature!

According to Galatians 5:15, what are some signs that you're allowing the old sinful nature to control you?

In Galatians 5:15, Paul pictured wild animals biting and hurting one another. It's terrible to see people acting that way—especially Christian. In verse 17 Paul explained how these things can happen.

> *For the flesh desires what is against the Spirit,*
> *and the Spirit desires what is against the flesh;*
> *these are opposed to each other, so that you*
> *don't do what you want.* —GALATIANS 5:17

Read Galatians 5:17 aloud. After hearing the verse, do you realize that your choices determine which nature will be in control of your life?

In Galatians 5:16, what must you do live in our new nature and allow it to affect your life. What is that condition?

Tomorrow you'll see more of what it means to walk in the Spirit.

DAY 2
You Belong to Your Choice

Read Galatians 2:20. When we refer to someone's "spirit," we mean the thoughts, motives, impulses, desires, and actions that person has. Until now, you've been a slave to the old nature. That nature has controlled your spirit and expressed itself through your body through sin and selfish pride.

But the word *Spirit* in Galatians 5:16 has a capital "S." When you became a Christ follower, Christ broke the old nature's control over your life. You now have a new nature. Christ in you controls your life through His Holy Spirit. The old nature sought to glorify itself; the new nature seeks to cause the love of God to flow through you.

Don't think of your new nature as "it." In Galatians 2:20 you are given the name of the One who is your new nature. What is that name?

According to this verse, complete the following sentence:

Since I have died with Christ, He now _____ within me!

Christ lives within you—what an awesome statement! You live by faith in the Son of God. You can remember what the word *faith* means in this way:

*F*orsaking

*A*ll

I

*T*rust

*H*im

What do you think Galatians 2:20 means by saying that you're to live by faith in the Son of God?

It's through your own choice that your new nature in Christ, can control your life. You must surrender yourself completely to Him. You must choose to let Him be your Lord and Master. And in making that decision, you belong to your choice. You become Christ's, not your own.

DAY 3

Under Christ's Control

Read Colossians 3:1-7. Quote from memory Galatians 5:22-23.
Remember: Christ lives in you. He *is* the new nature you have been given. We often, ask Christ to give us things like love, patience, gentleness, or righteousness. He doesn't give us these things; He *is* each one of those things! Instead of giving you the characteristics you desire, He has given you the source of those characteristics. This is your new nature. This is why the more deeply we know Christ, the more like Him we become.

The attributes of Christ, *your new nature,* are shown beautifully in the memory verse for this week, Galatians 5:22-23. Remember, you can use the ready-made cards from the back of this *Survival Kit*, an app, or homemade ones.

Read Colossians 3:1-7. Then turn back to Colossians 2:12-13. How does Colossians 2:12 shed light on the expression "risen" or "raised to life" Paul used in Colossians 3:1?

Remember, your baptism does not give you your new nature. You already have Christ living in you. Your baptism is only a symbol of what has happened to you. In the space above, did you write something like this? "My old life has been symbolically buried with Christ, and I have now been resurrected into a new life with Christ."

Three times in five verses Paul called on you to make a personal choice as a Christian—once in Colossians 3:1, again in verse 2, and a third time in verse 5.

How does your Bible state these three choices?

Verse 1:

Verse 2:

Verse 5:

...seek what is above, where the Messiah is, seated at the right hand of God....Set your minds on what is above, not on what is on the earth....Therefore, put to death what belongs to your worldly nature. —COLOSSIANS 3:1B,2,5A

Based on what you have learned from these verses, what commitment would you like to make for your life today?

DAY 4

Christ Within

Read 2 Corinthians 4:6-10. The following words have special meaning for you as a Christian; they have something to do with your new nature.

Controller   Container

Second Corinthians 4:6-10 uses different ways to describe your new nature. **Read those verses now. Which verse explains the new meaning of the word container as it applies to you? Verse _____**

Which word describes what is inside this container?

Because of the treasure within the container—Christ within your life— you'll experience victory. Second Corinthians 4:8-9 pictures this victory in a series of four comparisons.

How does your Bible phrase those four comparisons in verses 8-9? Write them here.

WE ARE	BUT WE ARE NOT

Here are the four comparisons you should have seen. Depending on your translation, they may use different words but have the same meaning.

WE ARE	BUT WE ARE NOT
pressured in every way	crushed
perplexed	in despair
persecuted	abandoned
struck down	destroyed

There's no doubt that becoming a Christian is an act by which you receive a new nature. The love of Christ can now control you instead of sin and brokenness. You're a container for a new life—the life of Christ. You are to be controlled by that life. You no longer live for yourself; you live for Christ. He has given you freedom to carry out His plans. Second Corinthians 4:7 compares your life to a clay pot, used in the New Testament to preserve valuable documents. The container was important because of what it contained. Of course, you are more than a clay pot. You are a person. God neither takes away your dignity nor expects you to become a puppet. Instead, Christ brings you to completeness.

DAY 5

Let Christ Be Lord

Read Galatians 5:22-25; Romans 8:28. Quote from memory: **Psalm 119:11; Romans 12:4-5; 1 Peter 4:10; and Galatians 5:22-23.**

Apple trees produce apples. They can't produce oranges, because by nature they're apple trees! Your new nature also produces fruit. That fruit is listed in a verse you should know by now: Galatians 5:22-23.

From memory write out Galatians 5:22-23 here:

Check your memory of Galatians 5:22-23. Notice that the fruit of the Spirit is not what you do, but what you are. In each case the fruit describes character, not activity.

Which of the nine fruits of the Spirit are impossible for you to live out on your own strength? The lack of which one in your life troubles you most as a new Christian? **Underline it in the verse you wrote down.**

New Christians often wonder how they can know that they've really become Christians. The answer to that question is based, first of all, on a fact: You have trusted your life to a trustworthy God. He promised that if you asked Him to forgive you of all your sins, He would do it. *You asked, and He did it. You can trust that He has forgiven you.*

Romans 8:28 states the result of your new nature taking control of your life. Take a minute to read Romans 8:28.

After reading Romans 8:28, mark the correct statement:

☐ **Everything turns out for good for people believe God exists and remain patient.**

☐ **God works everything out for good for people who love God and are called according to His purpose.**

If you marked the second statement, you're on the right track. God doesn't just let things happen; He takes active control of your life as you yield to Him through the indwelling Christ.

There is a simple decision you make as a Christian—hour by hour, day by day. It is to trust Christ with your life. When you do, His nature produces the fruit of the Spirit. This can be difficult, but will always be worth it.

TWO NATURES, PART TWO
THE OLD NATURE

WEEK FIVE

But now you must also put away all the following: anger, wrath, malice, slander, and filthy language from your mouth. Do not lie to one another, since you have put off the old self with its practices and have put on the new self. –COLOSSIANS 3:8-10A

DAY 1

Dethrone the King of Sin

Read Romans 6:12-18. Memorize Colossians 3:8-10a. Have you heard people say, "That's just human nature" as an excuse something bad they did? This excuse doesn't make sense for Christ followers. Christ doesn't let us get by with living according to human nature. He is your new nature, changing your attitudes and your actions.

Yet your human nature isn't dead. It's still there, like before you gave your life to Christ. **Read what Romans 6:12-18 says about your old nature.**

This passage shows sin as a sort of king, with the power to rule over you. Verse 12 says the choice is yours: If you "let sin reign," you must take the consequences.

Your old nature is your human nature. It is the nature of sin within you. It was not destroyed when you became a Christian. Rather, it was dethroned for the first time. For the first time, sin has no power to control your life... except when you choose to become a slave to it again. You belong to your choice.

CHECK TO SEE IF YOU UNDERSTAND:	
Who is the new nature within you?	
Who is the old nature within you?	
Who decides who will reign over you?	

Answers: 1. Christ; 2. yourself or sinful nature; 3. You must decide!

Do you remember a verse that tells one of the best ways to keep from surrendering to sin in your life? It was the first Scripture memory verse you were assigned in this *Survival Kit*. If you cannot remember look back in the front of the book. **Write the verse here.**

Be sure to check how accurately you quoted Psalm 119:11. Then look again at Romans 6:14-18. Remember that sin is dethroned but not dead.

You may choose to obey the sinful self, your old nature. Or, you may choose to obey Christ, your new nature. You're the slave of the nature you choose to follow.

DAY 2
No Reformation

Read Romans 7:15,18-21. One of the hardest things for a new Christian to realize is this: *Your old nature can't be reformed!* When you try to live in the old nature and produce the fruit of the new nature, you grow frustrated.

Romans 7:15,18-21 pictures a Christian who attempts to do this. Read the passage verses and summarize the struggle in your own words.

Did you write something like this? "I want to do good... but I can't do it! I don't want to do evil...but I do it!"

How does your own life relate to the struggles you just summarized?

Does it seem logical to you that you will still struggle with sin even after Christ has come to dwell in your life? Why or why not?

It may not seem logical, but it happens because your old nature can't be reformed. When you have apple roots, you produce apples. The nature of the root always determines the fruit. Your old nature is still producing the same kind of fruit as it did before you became a Christian.

Christians mistakenly assume that giving their life to Christ has automatically taken away everything that might ever lead them astray. They forget that this old nature still exists and can never be reformed.

DAY 3
Civil War Within

Read Romans 7:22-25; 8:5-6. Quote from memory Colossians 3:8-10. Would you believe that a civil war can go on in your life as a Christian? Such a war takes place when your new nature and your old nature struggle against each other. The struggle described in Romans 7:22-25 is caused by a Christian who has not made a clear-cut decision to let Christ be the Lord of his life. Romans 7:23 mentions a frequent result of war: captivity. And Romans 7:24 shows a hideous situation. Ancient conquerors developed a terrible way of torturing a prisoner. They would bind a corpse to him so tightly that the living man, if he tried to escape, would have to carry the dead man on his back!

In verse 24 the apostle Paul asked a question which shows he may have been thinking about this horrible torture. What is that question?

"Who will deliver me?" Paul pleaded. "Who will set me free?"

Romans 7:25 gives both the name and the title of the One who can release you from this civil war within. Write them both here.

Name: _____

Title: _____

What significance does this title have in bringing to an end the civil war between your two natures?

50

If Jesus Christ is truly your Lord, then He must control your life. You must own His lordship and refuse to obey your old human nature.

Look now at Colossians 3:8-10a, your memory assignment for this week. Notice that the portion to be memorized ends with the first part of verse 10, after "the new man" or "the new self" or "the new nature." Don't delay beginning to work hard on memorizing this passage. **Use the space below to write down what you can remember.**

Read Romans 8:5-6. These verses contrast two types of life which you may experience as a Christian—yielded to the old nature or yielded to the new nature. Complete this simple chart to show the contrast:

	THE OLD NATURE	THE NEW NATURE
Mind-set *(v. 5)*		
Results *(v. 6)*		

You should have completed the chart using similar words like this:

	THE OLD NATURE	THE NEW NATURE
Mind-set *(v. 5)*	things of the flesh	things of the Spirit
Results *(v. 6)*	death	life and peace

DAY 4
Victory Through Surrender

Read Ephesians 4:22-24; Matthew 5:21-22,27-28; Philippians 4:7-8; and Romans 8:37-39. Today's Bible readings may seem like a lot, but the total number of verses isn't that many. They just come from several different books of the New Testament.

Begin by reading Ephesians 4:22-24. These verses should remind you of Colossians 3:8-10, which you began memorizing Monday.

Write down Colossians 3:8-10a.

In both Colossians 3:8 and Ephesians 4:22, the writer referred to a deliberate decision made by a Christian to lay aside, or put off, the old nature. Think of a person who has been wearing a suit of clothes for a long time. As an intentional act, that person takes off his old clothes and throws them away. They're no longer valuable to the owner and won't to be worn again. Making this decision as new Christian begins settling the civil war within! The old nature is still present, but its power is rendered helpless by your decision to lay it aside. Your daily choice of a permanent commitment to Jesus Christ allows the full power of His life to be activated within you.

Colossians 3:8-10 lists many characteristics of the old nature. Which ones do you want to lay aside most?

In Ephesians 4:23, Paul referred to renewing your _____.

Read Romans 8:37. What happens when you make Christ the Lord and Master of your life?

As a believer, you become an overcomer in Him. Romans 8:38-39 continues the same thought, saying that nothing in all of creation can separate you from the love of God through Jesus Christ your Lord.

DAY 5

One Decision

Read Romans 6:1-11. Quote from memory Psalm 119:11; Romans 12:4-5; 1 Peter 4:10; Galatians 5:22-23; and Colossians 3:8-10.

Read Romans 6:1-2 to find out whether Paul allowed any excuse for your living as a Christian with your old nature still in control.

What unanswerable question did Paul ask in verse 2?

In Romans 6:3-5, Paul spoke of baptism as your public confession that something already has taken place in your life. What is that confession?

In baptism, you confess that your old sinful self is dead and that you now have been raised to new life in Christ.

According to Romans 6:6-7, what has happened to you to free you from the power of the old nature?

Paul said your old nature was crucified with Christ. How did Paul explain your life as a Christian (vv. 8-11)?

Here's one way to sum up what Paul said in Romans 6:8-11:

As far as sin is concerned, you're dead. As far as God is concerned, you're only alive in Jesus Christ.

Consider where you are as a new Christian. Have you ever felt really proud and confident about your ability to overcome temptation, but suddenly anger, frustration, resentment, or lust appeared in your life? Did you begin to question whether you were really Christian after all? Perhaps you felt embarrassed. You tried to act like you were a growing Christian, but you knew all the time it wasn't a real life you were living.

Following Christ doesn't consist of trying to be like Jesus. That's impossible. It's letting Jesus Christ, the Son of God, become the reigning King in your life, making you more like Him. You give Him the right to guide your thoughts, to control your hands. You settle once and for all the fact that He came into your life to be your Lord, the One to whom you belong.

SALVATION
ITS BEGINNING & COMPLETION

WEEK SIX

I am sure of this, that He who started a good work in you will carry it on to completion until the day of Christ Jesus. **—PHILIPPIANS 1:6**

DAY 1

Three Aspects of One Event

Read Philippians 1:3-11. Memorize Philippians 1:6. Maybe when your surrendered your life to Christ as your Lord and Savior, you thought that simple prayer of surrender would give you all Christ had to offer you. You were right!

In that moment, you were forgiven, freed, and made a Christ-indwelled child of God. In that same moment, however, you also received some rights from God. You were given an inheritance. Those rights are yours to claim in the present. That inheritance is yours to claim in the future.

Salvation, therefore, comes to you in three stages: past, present, and future. The apostle Paul knew this and explained it to his friends, the Philippian Christians. Read what Paul wrote in Philippians 1:3-11.

What did Paul do when he remembered his friends in Philippi? (v. 3)

When Paul thanked God for the Philippian Christians, what did he always feel when he prayed? (v. 4)

What did Paul specifically thank God for? (v. 5)

The Philippian Christians were Paul's partners in spreading the gospel. Where did he say he held them? (v. 7)

Paul's feelings of love and affection were so strong that he compared his emotions to the love and affection of whom? (v. 8)

Paul wanted to make sure that the Philippians understood three aspects of salvation. Note the time frames Paul used in the verse:

I am sure of this, that He who started a good work in you will carry it on to completion until the day of Christ Jesus. —PHILIPPIANS 1:6

How is your relationship with Christ helping you in your daily life? Reread Philippians 1:9-11 to start thinking about your response, then prayerfully write your answer during your quiet time.

DAY 2

Salvation Past

Read Ephesians 2:3-6,8-9,12-13,17-19. All the Scripture for today relates to *salvation past*: the moment when you prayed, asking Christ to enter your life as Lord and Savior.

Read Ephesians 2:3-6. What did God do at that moment you trusted Jesus Christ? Verse 5 explains it in two ways. Write them here.

1. _____
2. _____

God made you alive together with Christ, and He saved you by His grace.

Verse 6 gives two more descriptions of what God did in that moment. Write them both here.

1. _____
2. _____

God raised you up with Christ and made you sit in heavenly places in Christ Jesus.

According to verses 8-9, what can you do to deserve God's forgiveness?

If you understood Ephesians 2:8-9 clearly you wrote "Nothing" in the blank space.

Now read Ephesians 2:12-13. Summarize these verses. What does it mean to be far off and brought near?

Ephesians 2:17-18 makes the matter clear. To whom were you given instant and constant access at the moment you gave your life to Christ?

What Christ did for you in that single moment when you prayed and asked Him to enter your life is simply amazing! He called you out of a world where sin and self rule over your decisions and pleasures. He instantly forgave all the sin and wrong deeds you had ever done. He cleansed you and made you as though you'd never sinned. He placed His own life inside yours and made you a part of His kingdom. In a moment of time, you were forever set free from the worry of facing judgment for your sin, being found guilty, and be separated from God forever. Those things are forever settled. Nothing can take away your new life in Christ. You are His...forever!

DAY 3
The Trinity Living Within You

Read Romans 8:9-11; 1 John 4:12-16. Quote from memory Philippians 1:6. When you prayed to become a Christian, you agreed with God that your living to please yourself was sinful and wrong. You asked Jesus Christ to forgive you of all the sin piled up in your yesterdays. You invited Him to become your Lord.

Today's Scripture teaches that at that point in time, a significant thing happened.

Read Romans 8:9-11. Notice how the titles of the Trinity—God, Christ, and the Holy Spirit—are interchanged. How many of these titles of the Trinity can you find and list?

_____   _____

_____   _____

_____   _____

Notice that all these titles for the Trinity are used interchangeably. Romans 8:9 refers to all three persons of the Trinity; so does verse 11. (It may be hard for you to find a reference to God the Father in Romans 8:11. The phrase "He that raised up Christ from the dead" refers to God the Father.)

Now reread these verses again and note the constant use of the phrase _dwells in you_ or _lives in you_. When you gave your life to Christ, you received the fullness of the Trinity.

The point is this: The Trinity cannot be divided. When you received Christ, you received the Holy Spirit of God. At that moment He came to dwell in you, to live within your life.

Can you repeat Philippians 1:6 aloud right now?

Now read 1 John 4:12-16 carefully. How many persons of the Trinity are mentioned in these verses? Circle the correct number.

1   2   3

Of the three persons of the Trinity who are mentioned, how many of them are said in these verses to dwell, or live, in us or have been given or sent to us? Circle the correct number.

1   2   3

Did you find all three? The Son has been sent as your Savior and as the Savior of the world. The Spirit has been given to you. And God Himself dwells in you. What an amazing and mind-blowing truth: You're a container for the abiding, indwelling Son, Spirit, and Father. The Triune God is living in your life!

That's a finished act. It never needs repeating. Hebrews 13:5 assures you that He will never leave you or forsake you.

DAY 4

Salvation Future

Read Ephesians 1:13-14; 1 Peter 1:3-9,13. Ephesians 1:13 teaches that you received the Holy Spirit at the moment you gave your life to Christ. Read that verse now, along with Ephesians 1:14.

What important truth is found in verse 14?

The Holy Spirit, whom you received at the moment of *salvation past*, is just the "down payment" on much more that God has reserved for your inheritance. Ephesians 1:14 in the King James Version uses the word *earnest*. When a person purchases a house, he puts "earnest money" down on it. That cash is a pledge of the full amount due, to be paid at a future time when he takes the house as his personal possession.

It illustrates our *salvation future*! The "down payment" of your "inheritance" has already been paid: the Holy Spirit is the evidence of that down payment. One day Christ will take you to heaven to be with Him. He'll redeem His purchased possession. When He does, your salvation will be complete.

Now read carefully 1 Peter 1:3-5. Do these verses speak of your salvation past or your salvation future?

☐ **A. Salvation past**   ☐ **C. Both past and future**
☐ **B. Salvation future**   ☐ **D. Neither past nor future**

The correct answer, of course, is that these verses refer both to that which Christ has already done for you (salvation past) and to that part of your salvation that is still in the future. As you read your Bible in the years ahead, you will find many passages of Scripture like this one. Be alert to the three aspects of salvation.

Look at 1 Peter 1:6-9. Which of the three aspects of salvation do you see in these verses?

☐ **A. Salvation past**   ☐ **C. Salvation future**
☐ **B. Salvation present**   ☐ **D. All of these**

First Peter 1:6-9 refers to your faith in Jesus Christ, whom you have never seen with your physical eyes. This relates to *salvation past*, and refers to the trials you are going through now, that serve to prove the genuineness of your faith. This relates to *salvation present*. And it further refers to a coming day when the testing of your faith will result in praise and glory and honor. This relates to *salvation future*.

Verses 7 and 13 of 1 Peter 1 tell you the exact time when you will be given your future salvation. When is it?

When Jesus Christ returns at the end of time, you will receive your promised inheritance. In your prayer time with God, be sure to thank Him for His promise of *salvation future*.

How is your daily quiet time developing? It has been about 40 days since you began using your *Student Survival Kit*. If you are developing a daily discipline of prayer and Bible study, keep at it. But if you're struggling with developing this discipline, don't be discouraged. Every time you make time to spend time with God is worth it!

DAY 5

Free from the Old Nature

Read Romans 5:12; 6:23; 1 Corinthians 15:50-57; 2 Corinthians 5:1-9. Quote from memory Psalm 119:11; Romans 12:4-5; 1 Peter 4:10; Galatians 5:22-23; Colossians 3:8-10; and Philippians 1:6.

Now what will *salvation future* be like? What will salvation provide for you that you do not have now and that you will not have until Christ comes again? The Bible tells of your future inheritance.

Read Romans 5:12 and Romans 6:23. What two short, fatal words are connected in both of these verses?

_____ *and* _____

What's the connection between sin and death, according to Romans 6:23?

Will you ever be rid of that old nature, the nature of sin? Yes. Because of sin, death awaits every person. Only those who are alive when Christ comes will not know the sting of death. But a time is coming when you will be set free from the presence of the old nature.

Read 1 Corinthians 15:50-57. Write down the verse number(s) that correctly answer the question.

QUESTION	VERSE #
Which verses tell you that your future salvation will come at a point in time?	
Which verses connect death with sin?	
Which verse tells you that you cannot inherit the kingdom of God with the old nature still within you?	
Which verses assure you that you are guaranteed immortality, as the old nature will be removed?	
Which verse assures you that this is the work of Jesus Christ, not the result of your own "good deeds?"	

Answers: A: 51-52; B: 55-56; C: 50; D: 53-54; E: 57

Think about 2 Corinthians 5:1-9. Verse 1 describes our lives as though they were "houses" or "tents." Verses 2-4 describe us as "groaning" in our present "house."

In your opinion, which of the following answers best describes the reason for our groaning?

☐ **A. Christians have such hard times in this present life.**
☐ **B. Christians are terrified of dying.**
☐ **C. Christians desire to be set free from the old nature.**

Verses 2 and 4 make the right answer clear, right? In verse 8 the apostle Paul plainly said he had rather cast aside his body with its human nature, so he would be "at home with the Lord" (2 Cor. 5:8, NASB).

Write out the verses that you have learned about putting off the old nature (Col. 3:8-10).

SALVATION
A DAILY PROCESS

WEEK SEVEN

For if, while we were enemies, we were reconciled to God through the death of His Son, then how much more, having been reconciled, will we be saved by His life! –ROMANS 5:10

DAY 1

Salvation Present

Read Romans 5:6-11. Memorize Romans 5:10. Review the three aspects of salvation.

Salvation Past: By the blood of Christ, you're forever set free from the penalty of sin.

Salvation Present: Through the indwelling life of Christ, you're here and now set free from the power of sin.

Salvation Future: By the return of Christ, you will be forever set free from the presence of sin.

Christ has given you freedom from the power of sin right now.

Study Romans 5:6-9. Which aspect of salvation do these verses explain? In the middle of which verse does the passage move from salvation past to salvation future?

Romans 5:6-8 describes the greatness of God's love in sending Christ to die for us. This description of salvation past continues in verse 9 with the statement that "we have now been declared righteous by His blood" (Rom. 5:9). In the middle of that verse, the emphasis shifts to *salvation future*, when we will be saved from any further judgment of God.

Romans 5:10 also begins by speaking of *salvation past*: "we were enemies, we were reconciled to God through the death of His Son" (Rom. 5:10).

Which aspect of salvation does Romans 5:10 speak of?

According to Romans 5:10, who is the source of our salvation present?

Use the same verse to complete this sentence:

By Christ's death, I have received salvation past;
now through Christ's _____ ,
I daily receive salvation _____ .

Through Christ's life, you daily receive salvation present. *Salvation present* means that you can "exult in God." The word *exult* means "to leap about; to be extremely joyful."[1]

Can you list three things in your personal life that Christ has brought you—things that make you want to "exult in God"?

1. _____
2. _____
3. _____

No matter what you wrote that makes you joyful, never forget who brings these joys into your life. Romans 5:10 is a key verse to understanding *salvation present*, which you enjoy now because of Christ living in you.

DAY 2
Saved by His Life

Read Hebrews 2:14-15,18; 4:14-16. *Salvation present* is the result of your Christ living in you. He provides His power to set you free from the power of sin. But does Christ really understand your needs, your weaknesses, your temptations? Today's Scripture passages can help you realize that He does.

Read Hebrews 4:14-16. These verses picture Jesus in a way the Jewish people, or Hebrews, could understand easily. Hebrews had a high priest who went into the sanctuary and offered sacrifices so that sins could be forgiven.

The writer of Hebrews described Jesus as what kind of High Priest?

Jesus is our great High Priest, who has gone into the heavens—that is, into the presence of God (Heb. 4:14).

According to verse 15, how does this great High Priest feel about the temptations to sin that you encounter?

Why does He feel this way about them?

Jesus sympathizes with you; He's understands your weaknesses. Why? Because He too was tempted in every way that we are (Heb. 4:15). But notice the crucial difference between Jesus and everyone else who has ever lived: He was without sin (Heb. 4:15).

According to Hebrews 4:16, what are you able to do because Jesus sympathizes with your temptations?

Stop right now and go boldly and confidently to God's throne of grace. Ask God for the strength you need to resist temptation.

After your prayer, read Hebrews 2:14-15,18. According to the first part of verse 14, what did Jesus do so that He will understand you perfectly?

Jesus took part in humanity. He shared the same flesh and blood that you have.

How far did Jesus go to experience every single thing that all people endure? One clear, five-letter word in the middle of verse 14 will give you the answer.

In addition to becoming flesh and blood and enduring all that you might have to endure in life, Jesus actually shared the human experience of *death*! There is nothing in all your life span that He has not faced personally.

DAY 3
Victory in the Spirit

Read Ephesians 5:18. Quote from memory Romans 5:10. Christ was tempted in every way you might be, but didn't sin. He will not let you to be tempted beyond your ability. He will always provide a way to escape. He provides all the resources you need!

Read Ephesians 5:18.

It's important to know two things about the Greek word used in the original text of Ephesians 5:18, that's translated be *filled*.

1. *It's a verb expressing a continued action: "be being filled."*
2. *It's a verb that expresses an order or command.*

This isn't an optional feature of the Christian life. We're commanded to be continually filled with the Spirit.

Ephesians 5:18 commands you to be filled continually with the Spirit of Christ. This aspect of salvation is a daily process that reminds us that you're saved not only by the death of Christ, but also by the _____ of Christ.

Write Romans 5:10 here. This memory verse states this great truth.

Salvation present is guaranteed by Christ. He offers you an unending supply of His Spirit. Whenever you are thirsty, you need only come to Him and drink. Christ's Spirit will fill you with His life. When that has happened, others will recognize quickly that you are different. Your life will bless the lives of others. Are you thirsty? Come to Christ and drink!

DAY 4

Working Out What God Is Working In

Read Philippians 2:5-13; Hebrews 13:20-21. Christ, the Son of God, understands everything you face in your daily life. He experienced it all for your sake.

One of the clearest statements of this truth in all the Bible is found in Philippians 2:5-8. Read those verses now. (Verse 6 could be reworded this way: *Christ Jesus was in the form of God but did not think of equality with God as something He must hold on to.*)

What two words in verse 7 show Jesus' was willingness to experience anything you may experience in life?

_____ *and* _____

Did you write "servant" or "slave" in one of those blanks? Did you write "men" or "human" in the other blank?

What word, used twice in verse 8, tells you how far Jesus was willing to go to share the common experience of humanity?

Because of Jesus' voluntary sacrificial death, what has God done? Read Philippians 2:9-11; then summarize what God has done.

You could summarize the passage this way: *God has made Jesus higher than all and will cause all to confess that fact.*

What will "every tongue" confess, according to verse 11?

Read Philippians 2:12-13. Do those verses seem a bit odd or out of place, coming right after God has made every tongue confess that Jesus Christ is Lord? After God exalts Christ (who lives in you) to be the King of kings and the Lord of lords, explaining that every knee will bow before Him, we're told to "work out your own salvation with fear and trembling" (Phil. 2:12). What a strange thing to say.

But look again at Philippians 2:12. Why are we to work out our salvation with *fear and trembling*? It's not for fear of being punished by an angry God. It's about something else. Here's what it is: You don't want to look past God's blessing in your life. And you tremble to think of living your life without His presence being fully in charge of your personality. That is what propels you to pursue Christ.

DAY 5
Salvation Is Rescue

Read Colossians 1:9-14. **Quote from memory Psalm 119:11; Romans 12:4-5; 1 Peter 4:10; Galatians 5:22-23; Colossians 3:8-10; Philippians 1:6; and Romans 5:10.**

Salvation begins at a point in time, with confession of your sin and confession of Christ's lordship. It continues as a process of time, in which you are freed from sin's power by Christ's indwelling life. In a final future event Christ will liberate you from the old nature of sin within your life.

Read Colossians 1:9-14. Which of these verses describes salvation past, salvation present, and salvation future? Put the following Scriptures on the lines that indicate their descriptions.

☐ Colossians 1:10-11   ☐ Colossians 1:12   ☐ Colossians 1:13-14

Salvation past	
Salvation present	
Salvation future	

In Colossians 1:9, the apostle Paul said he was praying for a very important kind of knowledge. What kind was it?

God wants you to "be filled with the knowledge of His will." He wants you to understand how His salvation comes to you in three aspects—past, present, and future. He wants you to know the certainty of your salvation past, made possible by Christ's death on the cross. He wants you to know the assurance of your salvation present, as Christ's saving life gives you strength to resist temptations to sin. One very important truth has been saved until last in our study of the three aspects of salvation: Exactly what is "salvation"?

Imagine you are standing on the shore of a lake, and you see a man in the middle of the water. He's unable to keep himself afloat. He will die quickly if someone doesn't save him. What's the element that will kill him? Water. He will drown in water. To be "saved," he must be taken from the water.

Salvation is leaving our sinful self-owned life and receiving the redeemed Christ-owned life. *Salvation is God's act of rescuing you from a sinful, self-directed life.* First, at a point in time, He took you out of that state. Next, as a daily process, He makes it possible for you to live a Christ-directed life. Finally, in a future event, He will set you free permanently from the possibility of a self-owned life. That is salvation.

[1]s.v. "exult," *Merriam Webster's Collegiate® Dictionary*, 11th ed., (Springfield, MA: Merriam-Webster, Incorporated, 2005), 445.

AUTHORITY
THREE INADEQUATE SOURCES

But the unbeliever does not welcome what comes from God's Spirit, because it is foolishness to him; he is not able to understand it since it is evaluated spiritually. –1 CORINTHIANS 2:14

DAY 1

Four Sources of Authority

Read Colossians 2:1-4,8,20-23. Memorize 1 Corinthians 2:14.
Everybody sometimes feels a need to get to whoever or whatever is
the final authority. The boss. The person in charge. This week, you will
study three subtle and dangerous sources of authority. Next week, you'll
concentrate on the one true source of authority. Read the descriptions of
the four sources of authority.

Match each with the word it best summarizes.

A. Experience   B. Intellect   C. Scripture   D. Tradition

	1. A person determines truth by his ability to reason what is right or wrong, good or bad, and so on.
	2. A person determines beliefs according to what has been important to his family, ancestors, and so forth.
	3. A person determines truth according to what God reveals in written form. This knowledge is ultimate and complete.
	4. A person determines truth by listening to his senses, his feelings, and emotions.

Answers: 1. B; 2. D; 3. C; 4. A

**Read Colossians 2:1-4. In verse 2, Paul said that he desired wealth
for the Colossian Christians; what kind of wealth did he mean?**

a_____ of u_____

**In his desire that Christians have full assurance of understanding,
Paul told them in verse 3 that in "Christ Himself" they would find all
the treasures of _____ and _____.**

How many inadequate sources of authority did Paul mention in Colossians 2:8? Write here words from that verse that refer to each of them.

Intellect: _____

Tradition: _____

Experiences:_____

God gave you your mind, your intellect; He expects you to use it. God gives you experiences, and these may be meaningful. Some things are unchanging, regardless of passing centuries; some traditions—especially those based on the Scriptures—are worth preserving. But intellect, experiences, and tradition cannot become ultimate authority for faith.

DAY 2
Intellect, Reason, and Logic

Read 1 Corinthians 1:18-25; 2:6-14. Many people are determined to make their intellect the final authority in all matters. Some people cannot believe something that does not seem logical. In this way, a person can crown himself "god" of his life. He believes that his own intelligence is capable of making final judgments about truth and error, good and evil, right or wrong.

Paul confronted people who had made intellect their source of authority.

Read 1 Corinthians 1:18-25. Debating with anyone about what he believes rarely does any good. In fact, Paul even said that God has made foolish all the w_____ of the w_____. (v. 20)

Paul analyzed the way two ethnic groups of his day used the wisdom of the world. Read 1 Corinthians 1:22-25 and summarize it below.

Paul wasn't saying that the Christian faith is anti-intellectual—far from it. The apostle Paul himself had one of the most brilliant and highly educated minds of his century.

Read 1 Corinthians 2:6-8 to learn what kind of wisdom Paul taught. How did it differ from the wisdom of the world?

Paul did not accuse humanity of having too much wisdom, but rather too little. If they had acquired enough true wisdom, they would not have crucified the Lord Jesus Christ.

Read 1 Corinthians 2:9-11 to learn why people of the world did not understand who Jesus was and why He came. According to verse 11, who alone understands God's thoughts?

If only the Spirit of God understands the thoughts of God, how can anyone else understand them? We can begin to understand God because Christians have received the Spirit of God, who teaches us God's truth.

According to 1 Corinthians 2:14, why is it impossible for a person to find God through his own intellect?

The natural, worldly person (and that means anyone who has not committed his life to Christ) has not received the Spirit of God. So, when speaking with a person who holds to intellect as ultimate authority, you cannot depend on reason alone. You must ask God to use His Holy Spirit to create the kind of awareness that will prepare such a person to believe.

You should have found 1 Corinthians 2:14 familiar when you read it today. **Try reciting it from memory.**

DAY 3

Experiences, Visions, and Impressions

Read Deuteronomy 13:1-4; Colossians 2:18-19. Quote from memory
1 Corinthians 2:14.

From the beginning of time, people have founded religions on
personal experience. Making experiences their authority, they have
called upon others to share these experiences. A person who has not
had such experiences is considered inferior, spiritually substandard.

The problem of evaluating an experience is a very serious matter. If
someone tells you he has had a vision sent from God, how can you be
certain that what he is saying is true? Authority based on experiences
is a dangerous thing. That is why God has found a better way to reveal
Himself. He has given us a written record of truth. By it, you can judge
all the many experiences that people claim come from God.

You can find a good example of this in Deuteronomy, the fifth book
of the Bible.

**Read Deuteronomy 13:1-4. According to these verses, which is a sure
test of truth in the experience of a prophet or a dreamer?**

☐ whether the prophecy or dream comes true
☐ whether the prophet entices you to turn away from God

Even when someone can show you signs and wonders, even when his
predictions seem accurate, you must not listen to him if he lessens your
devotion to God.

**Read Deuteronomy 13:3. Why do those who make experiences their
religious authority seem so persuasive?**

Think again about problems caused by those who cling to experiences
as the source of religious authority.

Read Colossians 2:18-19. What specific problem did Paul write about?

Some of the Colossians apparently had experienced visions. As a result, they were trying to make all the Christians join them in worship of angels and in other false religious practices. **According to verse 19, what mistake is made by people who use experiences as their authority?**

The apostle Paul made a strong statement about those who lean on experiences as their authority: They do not hold fast to Christ, the Head of the church. Experiences do not tend to cement people together in a church. Instead, they tend to cause divisions. Those who have had a certain experience tend to look down on those who have not.

Be wary to those who encourage you to seek an experience. When God gives you a special time of fellowship, it can be a blessing. But when you begin to seek the experience rather than the fellowship with God, watch out. You may be "captured" by a false source of authority.

DAY 4

Tradition

Read Matthew 15:1-9. How do traditions develop? Someone in the past decided that a particular teaching or custom or ceremony should be repeated again and again. For that person, the teaching or custom or ceremony was extremely important. It had to be preserved. However, sometimes the meaning of the teaching or custom or ceremony is lost. A tradition becomes a dead ritual, bringing no help to people. It calls for no real heart commitment. Tradition can imprison people who might find the true meaning of the original teaching or custom or ceremony if it were expressed in some other way.

Read Matthew 15:1-9. Why were the religious leaders critical of Jesus' disciples?

Jesus' disciples broke with tradition by failing to wash their hands in a certain customary way before eating bread. But Jesus replied that these religious leaders themselves were ignoring a more important matter.

Which of the Ten Commandments did He accuse them of breaking?

In Matthew 15:6, which two of the four sources of religious authority does Jesus mention as clashing with each other?

_____ *VERSUS* _____

When it comes to Scripture versus tradition, you must make a choice. **Summarize in your own words the prophecy of Isaiah quoted by Jesus in Matthew 15:8-9.**

Some people give God lip service instead of heart service. They substitute man-made doctrines for God-given truths.

According to 1 Peter 1:18-19, can tradition bring salvation to people? Why or why not?

Tradition tends to become a matter of outward expression, not of the heart, and human traditions sometimes actually clash with God's Word.

DAY 5

Intellect, Experiences, and Tradition

Read 1 Timothy 1:3-7; 6:20-21; 2 Timothy 2:15-19. Quote from memory the eight Scripture passages you have learned up to this point.

As a new Christian, you will be exposed to lots of religious teaching. Many sincere people will present to you their systems of belief. Examine them carefully. Are they based on intellect? Are they based on experiences? Are they based on tradition?

Read 1 Timothy 1:3-7. What do man-made teachings lead to?

What does true teaching from God lead to?

What impure motives do false teachers have, according to verse 7?

"Teachers of the law" were people in places of honor. Some people today want to get honor and glory by teaching inadequate sources of authority!

Read 1 Timothy 6:20-21. What did the apostle Paul instruct Timothy to do with the truth he had been given from God?

If Timothy guarded and kept safe the true teaching, how was he to react to false teachers?

Paul warned Timothy to avoid false and foolish ideas. Read
2 Timothy 2:15-19 to see further instructions about false ideas.

Which false source of authority is mentioned in verse 16?

**Hymenaeus and Philetus turned away from Scripture to another source
of authority. Based on verses 16-18, which one do you think it was?**

Apparently intellect was the inadequate source of authority used by
these false teachers. Their teachings upset the faith of some people, but
the firm teachings from the Word of God stood strong (2 Tim. 2:18-19).

This week you used your *Student Survival Kit* to study three
inadequate sources of authority. But you have also been learning
from the very beginning that Scripture is your authority as a Christian.
What verse have you learned that tells what Christ has done for you?
Write Romans 5:10 here.

AUTHORITY
ONE TRUE SOURCE

WEEK NINE

All Scripture is inspired by God and is profitable for teaching, for rebuking, for correcting, for training in righteousness... –2 TIMOTHY 3:16

DAY 1

Sacred Scripture,
The Only Safe Authority

Read 2 Timothy 1:1-2,5; 3:14-17. Memorize 2 Timothy 3:16. Four sources of authority… but only one of them is trustworthy! The apostle Paul knew which one that was. **Read 2 Timothy 3:14-17.** Timothy had studied God's Word since he was a child, and knew it was able to give him wisdom, which leads to salvation through faith in Jesus.

Focus now on 2 Timothy 3:14. What did the apostle Paul instruct Timothy to continue doing?

What's the difference between learning a truth and believing that truth?

Firm belief or conviction in what you are taught comes more easily when the people who lead you also model those teachings in their lives.

Verse 14 says that Timothy knew who his teachers were. **Find three in 2 Timothy 1:1-2,5; record their names and relationship to Timothy.**

_____, who was Timothy's _____

_____, who was Timothy's _____

_____, who was Timothy's _____

Lois was Timothy's grandmother, and Eunice was Timothy's mother. What relationship did you list for Paul? In verse 2, Paul called Timothy his son, but he was using that word to explain their relationship. Paul became like Timothy's spiritual father, so he referred to him as his son.

Reread 2 Timothy 3:16. Who inspired the Scriptures?

Because God inspired the Bible, list what it's useful for?

_____   _____

_____   _____

Studying scripture, which is useful for teaching truth, rebuking error, correcting faults, and giving instruction for right living, will obviously have an effect on your life.

Focus on verse 17. What will you become as you study Scripture?

Do you really want to become fully qualified and equipped to do every good deed? You're doing it now if you are being faithful to consistently study God's Word, working through the study guides in your *Student Survival Kit*, and learning your Scripture memory verses. Do you still remember why it is so important to memorize God's Word? Recall Psalm 119:11.

Timothy had been studying the Scriptures from the time he was a child. You cannot begin your own lifetime of study any sooner than today. Make a commitment in prayer now, and give priority time to reading God's Word.

DAY 2
Scripture Before Experience

Read 2 Peter 1:16-21; Matthew 17:1-5. You have read many passages of Scripture written by Paul. You've found these passages in books of the Bible grouped in a section called Paul's Letters. Right after that section comes another section of New Testament books called General Letters. Two of those letters were written by the apostle Peter.

Read 2 Peter 1:16-18. In this passage, Peter referred to a remarkable event he had witnessed. That event was the transfiguration of Jesus Christ.

Read these statements Peter made:

_____"We were eyewitnesses of his majesty."
_____"He received honor and glory from God the Father."
_____"The voice was borne to him... 'This is my beloved Son, with whom I am well pleased.' "
_____"We heard this voice borne from heaven."
_____"We were with him on the holy mountain."

Now read the actual account of this event found in Matthew 17:1-5. In front of each of the statements above that Peter made, write the number of a matching verse from Matthew 17:1-5. (Some verses may be used more than once.) See how closely Peter's statements match what actually happened.

It is clear that Peter knew what he was talking about. He actually stood on the mountain that day with James and John and saw Jesus glorified. He heard the voice of God the Father from heaven. In 2 Peter 1:16, Peter stated his personal knowledge that this event in the life of Jesus Christ was not a "cleverly devised story." It really happened, and Peter was there to see it happen.

Read what Peter said next in 2 Peter 1:19-21 carefully. Notice he spoke of something being made more sure. What could be more sure than something that he had witnessed in person? Yet Peter said we're even more confident of the message proclaimed by the prophets (2 Pet. 1:19). In other words, Peter was saying, there's something even more trustworthy than what I saw and heard myself, the words written by men who were guided by the Holy Spirit of God.

In 2 Peter 1:20-21, the apostle Peter made two important statements about the things written in God's Word.

In your own words, write down what Peter said the Bible is not.
1. The Bible is not _____
2. The Bible is not _____

Peter stated that the Bible is not a private or individual interpretation of truth. It's not based on any single person's opinion, belief, or viewpoint. Nor is it the result of an act of human will. Instead, Scripture came about as the result of the activity of God. *God breathed upon men as they recorded God's truth.*

What principle can you set up for your own life as a result of Peter's teaching in this passage—a principle related to your final authority for matters of faith? **Pray about this question during your quiet time. List below any insight you gain.**

DAY 3
An Amazing Book

Read Micah 5:2; Matthew 2:1-6; 27:13-14,38,57-60; Isaiah 53:5,7,9; and John 14:2-3; 19:1,4,34; 20:25. Try to quote 2 Timothy 3:16 from memory.

The Bible is an amazing book containing hundreds of statements about events that had yet to happen when the writers recorded them. Prophecies about future kings and kingdoms, predictions of births and deaths, forecasts of the coming of the Savior into the world. All these are found in the pages of the Bible.

For example, read Micah 5:2 and Matthew 2:1-6. Where did the prophet Micah say the Savior was to be born? Where was Jesus born?

In about 740 B.C., the prophet Micah predicted that Jesus would be born in Bethlehem. Mary, Jesus' mother, lived in Nazareth, but because of an order from the Roman government, she had to travel to Bethlehem. That's why she was there when Jesus was born. At the time that Mary conceived, even she couldn't have guessed that this would happen.

Next, read a part of an incredible prophetic poem: Isaiah 53:5,7,9. The passage is divided properly into poetic lines, marked here as subdivisions of the verses (like 5a, 7b, and so on).

^{5a} *He was pierced through for our transgressions,*
^{5b} *He was crushed for our iniquities;*
^{5c} *The chastening for our well-being fell upon Him,*
^{5d} *And by His scourging we are healed.*
^{7a} *He was oppressed and He was afflicted,*
^{7b} *Yet He did not open His mouth.*
^{9a} *His grave was assigned to be with wicked men,*
^{9b} *Yet with a rich man in His death;*
^{9c} *Although He had done no violence,*
^{9d} *Nor was there any deceit in His mouth.*

—ISAIAH 53:5,7AB,9 NASB

Now read the New Testament verses listed below. Beside each one, write the number and letter of one or more verse subdivisions from Isaiah 53 (such as 5a or 9c). See how accurately the prophet predicted facts about Jesus' trial, suffering, crucifixion, death, and burial.

	John 19:34		Matthew 27:14
	John 20:25		Matthew 27:38
	John 19:1		Matthew 27:57-60
	John 19:4		Matthew 27:13

John 19:34: 5a; John 20:25: 5b; John 19:1: 5d; John 19:4: 9c, 9d; Matthew 27:13: 7a; Matthew 27:14: 7b; Matthew 27:38: 9a; Matthew 27:57-60: 9b

Hopefully, this has given you a new respect and an awe for the mystery and power of God's Word. Many biblical prophecies already have come true. This is why you can be confident that the others eventually will be fulfilled as well.

DAY 4

An Eternal Source of Wisdom and Righteousness

Read Psalms 19:7-11; 37:29-31; 119:89-91,98-101. What does the Bible say about itself? The Bible says it's an eternal source of wisdom and righteousness.

Before opening your Bible, read these two explanations: (1) *In the verses to be studied today, you will find many different expressions for the Word of God, such as law, precepts, testimonies, statutes, commandments, and judgments.* (2) *The expression "Word of God," as used in the Bible, has a broader meaning than the Bible alone. It means anything God says about Himself, whether through the voice of His prophets or through the majesty of His creation or through the ordering of human history in His world.* "The Word of God" means the active expression of God's very nature. As such, it certainly includes the Scriptures—those writings that are the unique record of God's activity. Now read carefully each of the verses listed at the beginning of this day's reading. These verses focus on three great claims the Bible makes about itself: that it is eternal, that it is a source of wisdom, and that it is a source of righteousness.

Beside each of the following key words, write the reference for each verse you read in which the Bible makes that claim for itself.

Eternal: _____

Wisdom: _____

Righteousness: _____

Do your completed lists look like these?

Eternal: Psalms 19:9; 119:89-91
Wisdom: Psalms 19:7; 119:98-100
Righteousness: Psalms 19:8-9,11; 37:29-31; 119:101

In addition to the verses you have read today, you also have been learning another passage in which the Bible makes statements about itself.

Can you remember it? (2 Tim. 3:16) Record it in the space below:

Another verse you have learned explains why many people misunderstand the Bible. The Bible was inspired by the Spirit of God and is interpreted correctly by people who are indwelled by the Spirit of God.

Quote a verse stating this fact (1 Cor. 2:14).

DAY 5
Four Sources of Authority? Or One?

Read 1 Corinthians 15:3-7 and Acts 18:24. Quote from memory Psalm 119:11; Romans 12:4-5; 1 Peter 4:10; Galatians 5:22-23; Colossians 3:8-10a; Philippians 1:6; Romans 5:10; 1 Corinthians 2:14; and 2 Timothy 3:16.

Four sources of authority exist, but only one of them is trustworthy. You know which one that is. Paul also knew which source of authority is trustworthy. **Read what Paul wrote in 1 Corinthians 15:3-7.** Paul mentioned the authority he was using for his summary of the death, burial, and resurrection of Jesus Christ twice.

Which source of authority was it?

Can you use the same authority Paul used when sharing Christ's life with others? Yes_____ No_____ Why or why not?

Yes, you also can use the Scriptures as your source of authority when you share Christ's life with others. But this doesn't "just come naturally" to you as a Christian.

Read in Acts 18:24,28 a short biography of a Christian man named Apollos. How do you think Apollos became so skilled in his knowledge and use of the Scriptures?

Is it important to you to know the Scriptures as well as Apollos knew them? Why or why not?

Is it important enough to rearrange your own personal priorities in order to study the Scriptures as Apollos must have studied them? Why or why not?

What areas of your life might have to be "rearranged" to provide the needed time for a lifetime habit of daily Bible study?

In all honesty, are you ready and willing to do that rearranging at this time? Yes_____ No_____ Explain your answer.

During these nine weeks, you have read and studied dozens of Bible verses. When you have completed your *Student Survival Kit*, don't break the habit of personal Bible study. If you will continue to use this same time daily for the rest of your life, you will soon become like Apollos!

Within the body of Christ, you will find those who have a special ability to put the deepest knowledge about the Bible into words. Cultivate friendship with them. They will bless your life! But at the same time, don't forget: Study the Word. Memorize the Word. Meditate on the Word. From it, your future growth as a Christian will develop.

THE 5 & 5 PRINCIPLE
IN PRAYER

Don't worry about anything, but in everything, through prayer and petition with thanksgiving, let your requests be made known to God. –PHILIPPIANS 4:6

DAY 1

The 5 & 5 Principle

Read Philippians 4:6 and memorize it. Look at your left hand. Use the fingers on that hand to count five people in your life who won't let you share your new faith with them. They may even make fun of you for your new relationship with God. You may really want to share your new life with them so that they may also enjoy it. But they will not even listen to you talk about Jesus Christ. What can you do? *Pray for them!*

Now look at your right hand. Count on those fingers five people in your life who will let you to share your new faith with them. Although they're not ready to place their lives in Christ's control, they are curious about the change they observe in you. They may even ask you questions about what you believe and why you believe it. What can you do? *Share with them!*

Next week your Bible study will focus on *witnessing*, a "Christian-ese" term that simply means telling other people how to have a relationship with Jesus. It is also called "sharing your faith." But the power of prayer is just as important as talking to others about Jesus because it can work with both those who will and those who will not let you share Christ with them. A great Christian once said: "You can do more than pray, after you have prayed. *But you can do no more than pray—until you have prayed!*"

In the space below, write down what you think that means:

Look now at Philippians 4:6. If you read the King James Version, use the word "anxious" in place of the word "careful." According to this verse, what is the alternative to being anxious about any situation you face in life?

What limits does this verse place on the things we can pray about?

As a Christian you can talk to God in prayer about everything, there is no limitation. Prayer is nothing more than talking with God. Sometimes you talk. Sometimes you listen. It is an opportunity for Christ to make your heart more like His, and meet needs. The answer to your prayers doesn't depend on your power in prayer but on His power to work in your life. That means praying for your unbelieving friends who won't allow you to share Christ with them is simply inviting Christ to work in their lives in spite of their attitude toward you.

Use the statements below to prepare for using the 5 & 5 Principle in your life. After the first statement, thoughtfully list the names of five people who currently won't allow you to share your faith with them. After the second statement, prayerfully list the names of five people who will permit you to talk with them about your new life in Jesus Christ.

THESE FRIENDS REFUSE TO LET ME SHARE CHRIST WITH THEM.	THESE FRIENDS ARE OPEN TO MY SHARING CHRIST.

DAY 2

A Little Faith Is Enough

Read Matthew 17:20; 21:21-22; James 1:5-8; and John 6:37.
As you think about praying for the salvation of your friends, do the
verses you have just read in Matthew and James discourage you?

**Describe below how you feel regarding these verses and prayer
for others:**

Perhaps you have written something like, "If my faith isn't strong
enough, I won't get any answers to my prayers. So, prayer is not for me;
I'm honest enough to admit I have a weak faith."

Read the words of Jesus in John 6:37:

> *The one who comes to Me I will
> certainly not cast out.* (NASB)

How much faith do you need to have before Jesus answers your
prayers? Jesus said that even faith as small as a mustard seed is
enough (Matt. 17:20). If you can go to Jesus with your need, it's enough!
He promised He will honor such faith. He won't cast out anyone who
trusts Him.

If you have enough faith to come to Jesus with your inability to help
yourself, He will deal with your doubts. Don't feel your faith is so weak
it would do no good to pray. Remember: *Prayer is simply letting Christ
use His power to work in an area of need, mold your heart to be more
like His, and to speak in the life of another.*

If your faith in Jesus is just large enough to ask Him to use His
power and to reveal Himself to the ten people you listed in yesterday's
work, then it's large enough. The greatest faith in the world is the one
that admits its limits and then leaves everything to Jesus. Don't be afraid
you will limit His power by your faith. Pray! It is no more complicated than

giving your Lord access to an area of need in your life. Just let yourself go in your prayer times, as Philippians 4:6 encourages you to do. (Have you memorized that verse yet?)

Write Philippians 4:6 here:

The only way you'll discover the power of prayer in reaching the seemingly unreachable people in your life is to pray for them. Today, think of each of the 5 & 5 you listed yesterday. One by one, turn them over to Jesus. Pray about a specific area of need in each life. Invite Jesus to enter that area of need with His power. Then wait for the results of your praying. God has His own timetable for answering...and He will answer!

DAY 3

Three Aspects of Prayer

Read Matthew 7:7-11. Quote from memory Philippians 4:6. In previous weeks, you learned about three aspects of your salvation: *past, present, and future.* Today, you will learn about three aspects of prayer. Each one of them have to do with your present fellowship with God.

What memory verse assures you it is useful or profitable to have daily time with God through His Word? (2 Tim. 3:16) Write it out below from memory and then check your answer in Scripture.

Now read Matthew 7:7-8. Often we describe praying as the action of "talking with God." These verses from Matthew describe praying as three actions. In the three verbs used, you can see three aspects of prayer.

List below these three actions. Then record God's response to that action beside each.

	ACTION	RESPONSE
1		
2		
3		

Meditate on the three verbs or action words used in Matthew 7:7-8.

Asking involves requesting something that you already know about: "Lord Jesus, I ask You to bring my friend to know Your love." You already know about Christ's love; you simply want it to be known by your unbelieving friend.

Seeking, on the other hand, involves requesting an answer about something you do not know about: "Lord Jesus, show me what I can do to express Your love to my friend. I don't know what to do next!"

Knocking involves asking Christ to enter an area of need that is behind closed doors: "Lord Jesus, tragedy in my friend's life has closed him off to Your love. Open the door to that area of need in him and show him how You can help him."

Read Matthew 7:9-11. These verses make several comparisons. List the comparisons and then circle the most important one.

The most important comparison in Matthew 7:9-11 does not involve bread or stone, a fish or a snake. Rather, the most significant metaphor is the comparison of a human father's integrity and compassion with the Heavenly Father's. If human fathers give their children what ask for, how much more likely is it that our Heavenly Father will give what we ask for?

DAY 4

Prayer Is Important

Read Matthew 14:23; Mark 1:35; and Luke 6:12; 22:39-41.

The apostle Paul knew that prayer is important.

Write down what Paul said that proves he knew the importance of prayer. (Phil. 4:6)

According to the verses you just read, where did Jesus go to pray? (You should be able to list three places.)

1._____ 2._____ 3._____

What times of day did Jesus choose for His prayer times? List the two you see.

1._____ 2._____

Jesus prayed in the hills, at a lonely or solitary place, and on the Mount of Olives. He prayed at night and before daybreak.

In your opinion, why did Jesus choose such times and places for prayer?

Luke 22:41 should have gives a clue to answering that last question. Jesus withdrew "about a stone's throw" away from His disciples (Luke 22:41, NASB). He chose times and places when He could be alone with His Father.

Luke 6:12 tells us that Jesus sometimes prayed the whole night through. Think about what this means. Jesus lived in constant prayer fellowship with God the Father, but He still needed to withdraw from the pressures of life, at regular times and at special places, in order to pray. Sometimes He even prayed for hours at a time. If the Lord

Jesus found it necessary to make a habit of prayer, how about you? Would you also benefit from doing so?

Look at your left hand. Think about the 5 & 5 Principle. What do you think would happen if you spent focused time in prayer for your five "unreachable" friends?

DAY 5
Prayer Brings Power to Win

Read John 14:13-14; Matthew 28:18-20. Quote from memory **Psalm 119:11; Romans 12:4-5; 1 Peter 4:10; Galatians 5:22-23; Colossians 3:8-10a; Philippians 1:6; Romans 5:10; 1 Corinthians 2:14; 2 Timothy 3:16; and Philippians 4:6.**

Are you already putting the 5 & 5 Principle to work in your life? Are you praying specifically for five people who will not let you share Christ with them? Are you asking, seeking, and knocking in your prayers as you invite Christ into their areas of need?

Read what Jesus said in John 14:13-14. Each of those verses tells you to ask in a certain way as you pray. The instructions are given twice.

You are to make your requests in the name of _____. What do you think that means?

When you make your requests in the name of Jesus, whose power is released to work?

God the Father, who is all-powerful, will be glorified in Jesus His Son as you pray in Jesus' name.

Now read Matthew 28:18-20. According to verse 18, how much power does Jesus have?

"All power is given unto Me in heaven and in earth." What an awesome statement! And what an awesome power is at your disposal through praying in Jesus' name!

(Here's a helpful hint: Matthew 28:18-20 will be the memory verse for next week. It is also the longest verse for memorization you have been given in your *Student Survival Kit*. You can get a good start memorizing on it over the weekend.)

Learn a lesson of the 5 & 5 Principle. Have you decided during this week that it is easier to pray for the five who are open to your sharing than for the five who are opposed to talking about God? Perhaps you think those who are the most resistant to a relationship with Christ will be the last to come to receive Christ as Savior and Lord because they are the hardest to reach.

We must reject the idea that the five on your left hand are harder for Christ to reach than the five on your right hand! What you think is "hard" and "easy" looks completely different to God. Such conclusions on your part only hinder your prayer life. When you pray in the name of Jesus for these friends, the One you are inviting to enter their lives has all power in heaven and on earth.

Saul of Tarsus was a powerful, murderous opponent of Christianity. No one could witness directly to him. He was hateful and destructive to Christians. Yet, the power of Christ transformed Saul in a powerful and unexpected way. In fact, Saul later became known as Paul, who wrote a good portion of the New Testament!

Do not underestimate the power of your prayers for the five who are difficult to reach. When you ask the Lord to enter our lives and needs through asking, seeking, and knocking, never doubt His ability to do what you ask. He can do more in a moment than we can do in a lifetime. In His name rests all the power there is in the entire universe.

THE 5 & 5 PRINCIPLE
IN WITNESSING

Then Jesus came near and said to them, "All authority has been given to Me in heaven and on earth. Go, therefore, and make disciples of all nations, baptizing them in the name of the Father and of the Son and of the Holy Spirit, teaching them to observe everything I have commanded you. And remember, I am with you always, to the end of the age." –MATTHEW 28:18-20

What It Means to Witness

Read Matthew 28:18-20 and memorize it. Five you can win through prayer alone; five you can win through telling people about how to have a right relationship with God—that's the 5 & 5 Principle.

For the rest of your life, keep the ten fingers of your two hands full. As long as you serve Christ, always have five people you are praying for and five people with whom you are sharing your faith. You will find that talking to five people and praying for five others at the same time is a full-time job for a believer!

The word *witness* comes from a Greek word, *maturia*. Look closely. Does it look like the English word *martyr*? Many of those who first shared their faith in Christ died for doing so, thus giving that meaning to the word *martyr*. The basic meaning of the word, however, is someone who shows evidence.

In the space provided, jot down a reason why you think "showing evidence" describes sharing your faith.

Witnessing isn't preaching. It's not even teaching the Bible. It is giving evidence. You have come to believe in Christ as your Savior and Lord. As a result, He lives in your life. You've prayed continually for His Spirit to fill you. As a result, your life is somehow different—in a positive way. It's evident to others who are near you. You are a witness because your life is bearing evidence to those who live around you. It's not so much something you do as it is the natural result of Christ living in you and flowing His love through you.

Shortly before Jesus left this earth (in bodily form) and returned to heaven, He stated to His followers a great claim, a great command, and a great promise. All three of these are found in Matthew 28:18-20, your memory selection for this week. Since you were given a helpful hint toward the end of last week, you already may be able to **write it here from memory.**

Try to do so now. If you can't do that yet, copy it carefully from whatever translation you are using for memorization.

Now circle the great claim that Jesus stated in Matthew 28:18-20. You studied this claim last week as you were learning about the great power of prayer.

If you found the great claim Jesus stated in the first part of Matthew 28:18-20, you should be able to find the great promise Jesus stated in the last part of those same verses. **Underline it.** Everything in between is the great command that Jesus gave to all His followers. Sometimes it is called "The Great Commission." You will learn more about this command in the coming days.

DAY 2
Christ Empowers Your Witness

Read Ephesians 5:18; Acts 2:1-18. Since beginning to use this *Student Survival Kit*, you have memorized many passages about the Holy Spirit.

What comparison is made in both of the above passages?

Both Ephesians 5:18 and Acts 2:13-18 compare drinking wine with being filled with the Holy Spirit.

Now read the whole story in Acts 2:1-18. What was the essential ingredient in the witness of those Christians?

Did you write that the filling of the Holy Spirit was the essential ingredient?

Now read the two statements below carefully. Think again about Acts 2:1-18. Mark which statement is correct.

- ☐ The Holy Spirit simply gave those people a new inner experience and did not expect them to verbalize it. It was enough for them to bear a "silent witness."
- ☐ The first act of the Holy Spirit, upon filling those people, was to make it possible for them to speak their witness to unbelievers so that every single person there would hear about Christ.

What's the result of a person being filled with the Spirit of Christ?

The result is *speaking*, not *silence*! For you as a person controlled by Christ dwelling in you, what will witnessing involve?

- ☐ Living for Christ without speaking about Christ.
- ☐ Speaking about Christ without living for Christ.
- ☐ Both living for Christ and speaking about Christ.

Someone said, "The greatest hypocrite in the world is the one who says, 'I don't have to talk to others about Christ; all they have to do is observe my actions, and they will know I am a Christian.'"

What is the problem with this statement?

First, this statement is just prideful. Second, it disregards the command of Jesus for us to share our faith. "But," you say, "what is there in my life that would be important to an unbeliever? I know only a few basics about the Christian life. I need to wait until I know more about God and the Scriptures before I can be a good witness." You've already passed from death to life. Christ's Spirit already lives in you and fills you constantly on request. *Remember: A witness is one who gives evidence.* You have much to give evidence about as Christ lives through you.

Five of your friends are open to your sharing. They are curious. Don't be afraid! Talk about what has happened in your life. Share the daily journey with Christ that you're now experiencing.

Share it in conversation with the five who are open to your testimony. Do it today.

DAY 3
Verbalizing Your Witness

Read Romans 1:16; Acts 22:1-15; 26:9-20. Quote from memory Matthew 28:18-20.

You have the evidence of a changed life—of the indwelling Christ controlling your life. You need to verbalize that witness, to tell people who Christ is and what He has done and how much He means to you now.

The apostle Paul knew how to verbalize what he believed about Jesus. Furthermore, he did so at every opportunity, to everyone who would listen. Read aloud these words that Paul once wrote:

> *For I am not ashamed of the gospel, for it is the power of God for salvation to everyone who believes.* —ROMANS 1:16A (NASB)

Can you honestly make the same statement Paul made? In the space provided, list reasons why you might feel ashamed about your faith.

Read now Acts 22:1-15 and Acts 26:9-20. Notice that in each case
Paul used his own conversion experience as the evidence he gave in
witnessing. In both instances, he mentioned four things about it. These
four things are listed and numbered in the following chart. In Acts 22:1-15
and in Acts 26:9-20 Paul verbalized his witness about these four things
in the same order they are numbered on the next page.

**In the correct column, write the references of two to four consecutive
verses from Acts 22 in which Paul told about each of four parts of
his conversion experience. Then do the same thing with the other
recorded time when Paul spoke his witness in Acts 26. You should be
able to find each of these four in no less than two or more than four
verses in a row. The first one in each column has already been filled
in for you.**

PAUL'S CONVERSION EXPERIENCE	ACTS 22	ACTS 26
1. Paul had not always followed Christ.	vv. 3-5	vv. 9-12
2. God began to deal with Paul's rebellion.		
3. Paul received Christ as Lord.		
4. Paul's new life was centered on Christ's purposes.		

Answers—Acts 22: vv. 3-5, vv. 6-9, vv. 10-13, vv. 14-15. Acts 26: vv. 9-12, vv. 13-18, v. 19, vv. 19-20.

You will be amazed to discover that most unbelievers have never heard
anyone share information of the type Paul shared in verbalizing his
witness! Every conversion experience is unique. Therefore, your own
testimony of how you came to know Christ is personal and individual.
It is evidence that no one but you can give. No one else will ever
duplicate it. And no one else can deny it!

DAY 4

The Personal Touch

Read Matthew 9:10-13; 1 Corinthians 9:19-23. It probably hasn't been
too long since you became a Christian.

As you thought about giving your life to Christ, who had a big influence on you?

Now read Matthew 9:10-11. What criticism did people make of Jesus?

Why did Jesus risk criticism by having personal contact with evil people? Read Matthew 9:12-13 before answering.

Jesus came to call sinners to repentance. He had mercy or compassion on those who were spiritually sick.

Now read what the apostle Paul wrote in 1 Corinthians 9:19-21. Which of these is what Paul meant?

□ A. It doesn't matter who I associate with.
□ B. I agree with whoever I'm with at the time.
□ C. I deliberately cultivate the friendship of all sorts of people.

Sentence C fairly states Paul's approach to making friends.

Why did Paul feel such a philosophy of life was necessary? Read 1 Corinthians 9:22-23 before answering.

Paul made friends with all sorts of people so that he could reach all sorts of people! Paul knew that not everyone whose friendship he developed would accept Christ, but he was willing to befriend anyone and everyone so that he could by all means save some (1 Cor. 9:22). He knew that God's power would save anyone who believed.

Interestingly enough, *Acts does not give a single instance where a person came to know Christ without the aid of a Christian!* Christ sent

Peter to a Roman soldier. He sent Philip to an Ethiopian official. He sent Paul to Lydia and her friends, to the jailer at Philippi, and to many others. *God uses people to reach people.*

Look again at your right hand. Those five people are open to your sharing with them. You should give time to them. Share your life with them. They have few other godly sources they can turn to and see a picture of God's grace because of the gospel. As you share your life with them, they will see Christ in your words, life, and thoughts. Seeing Christ dwell in you will have a tremendous impact on them.

Once again, priorities need to be kept straight! Take another look at your weekly schedule. **Is there time for those five people?**

If not, what can you put lower on your schedule of priorities to make room for them? Pray about your answer during your daily quiet time.

Look now at your left hand. Are you still remembering to pray for those five people who at present are not open to your witness?

DAY 5
Pray and Witness

Read Matthew 18:19-20; Acts 2:41-47. Quote from memory Psalm 119:11; Romans 12:4-5; 1 Peter 4:10; Galatians 5:22-23; Colossians 3:8-10a; Philippians 1:6; Romans 5:10; 1 Corinthians 2:14; 2 Timothy 3:16; Philippians 4:6; and Matthew 28:18-20. Congratulations on memorizing so much Scripture!

Most things about the Christian life are better caught than taught.

Read Matthew 18:19-20. Verse 20 speaks of how many people being gathered together in the name of Christ? Verse 19 contains what great prayer promise made by Jesus?

Where even two or three people gather in Jesus' name, He promises to be with them. When two people agree on a request to be prayed for in Jesus' name, He promises to grant it.

What does this mean to you as you look at your two hands and think of those ten people who do not yet know Jesus Christ as Lord and Savior? Has someone come into your life who is a more mature Christian than you are—someone you can join in prayer for salvation of your 5 & 5? Yes_____ No_____

If so, who?

If not, who might be a good mentor for you?

Remember: Most things about the Christian life are better caught than taught. Your growth as a Christian will be strengthened as you associate with others who have had more time to grow than you.

Read now some verses you read several weeks ago when you studied about the one body of Christ, the church: Acts 2:41-47. Those early Christians didn't try to "go it alone," did they? They shared everything they had; they shared their very lives with their fellow believers in the body of Christ. Your fellow believers can help you grow. And they can help equip you to share your faith with others.

Can you imagine what an impact would be made on the world if every Christian were to commit time to reaching ten people constantly, using this 5 & 5 Principle?

Your journey has just begun. The Scripture passages you have studied and the verses you have memorized are only the beginning of your learning; you will discover much more about your inheritance, your rights, and your privileges as a child of God. From those of us who are your older brothers and sisters in the body of faith, hear our hearty greeting:

Welcome, friend! Enter with us into all Christ has reserved for us...together.

WHERE DO YOU GO FROM HERE?

For the past 11 weeks, this book has been your companion as you have learned some important truths about the Christian life.

One of the first truths you learned is the importance of being a part of the body of Christ. To thrive spiritually, it is essential that you be surrounded by others who are concerned about your spiritual growth. If you have not already joined a church and become connected to a Bible study, small group, or ministry, it's time to do so at once. God made us to live in community with other believers. Without community, we will not grow in the peace and joy God has designed us for.

You also have established some disciplines that are important to your spiritual growth: Bible reading, prayer, and Scripture memory. You should continue with the disciplines. These habits are essential to your continued spiritual growth. Do do not neglect them.

Although memorizing Scripture has been difficult, you probably have found it to be rewarding. Each week select one or more verses from your Scripture readings. Make your own cards from index cards or from heavy paper. Continue to memorize and review.

The 5 & 5 Principle has taught you to pray for persons who need to come to know Christ. Begin using the same kind of intercessory prayer for persons who have other needs.

NOTES

NOTES

NOTES

ESSENTIAL
TEEN STUDY BIBLE

ESSENTIAL
TEEN STUDY
BIBLE

INCLUDES 146
ESSENTIAL
CONNECTION
DEVOTIONS

HCSB

The HCSB Essential Teen Study Bible can give teens all the tools needed to tackle this life and learn to live it God's way. Filled with hundreds of study helps and 146 devotions written especially for teens, this fully designed, four-color Bible will help them apply God's Word each day and connect with Him as never before.

WEEK 5

Two Natures, Part Two
The Old Nature

But now you must also put away all the following: anger, wrath, malice, slander, and filthy language from your mouth. Do not lie to one another, since you have put off the old self with its practices and have put on the new self. **—COLOSSIANS 3:8-10A**

WEEK 6

Salvation
Its Beginning and Completion

I am sure of this, that He who started a good work in you will carry it on to completion until the day of Christ Jesus. **—PHILIPPIANS 1:6**

WEEK 3

One Body
Its Service

Based on .the gift each one has received, use it to serve others, as good managers of the varied grace of God. **—1 PETER 4:10**

WEEK 4

Two Natures, Part One
The New Nature

But the fruit of the Spirit is love, joy, peace, patience, kindness, goodness, faith, gentleness, self-control. Against such things there is no law. **—GALATIANS 5:22-23**

WEEK 1

The Indwelling Christ

I have treasured Your word in my heart so that I may not sin against You. **—PSALM 119:11**

WEEK 2

One Body
Its Life

Now as we have many parts in one body, and all the parts do not have the same function, 5 in the same way we who are many are one body in Christ and individually members of one another. **—ROMANS 12:4-5**

WEEK 6
Salvation
*Its Beginning
and Completion*

—PHILIPPIANS 1:6

WEEK 5
Two Natures,
Part Two
The Old Nature

—COLOSSIANS 3:8-10A

WEEK 4
Two Natures,
Part One
The New Nature

—GALATIANS 5:22-23

WEEK 3
One Body
Its Service

—1 PETER 4:10

WEEK 2
One Body
Its Life

—ROMANS 12:4-5

WEEK 1
The Indwelling Christ

—PSALM 119:11

WEEK 11
The 5 & 5 Principle
In Witnessing

Then Jesus came near and said to them, "All authority has been given to Me in heaven and on earth. Go, therefore, and make disciples of all nations, baptizing them in the name of the Father and of the Son and of the Holy Spirit, teaching them to observe everything I have commanded you. And remember, I am with you always, to the end of the age."
—MATTHEW 28:18-20

BONUS SCRIPTURE
God's Love

For I am persuaded that not even death or life, angels or rulers, things present or things to come, hostile powers, height or depth, or any other created thing will have the power to separate us from the love of God that is in Christ Jesus our Lord!
—ROMANS 8:38-39

WEEK 9
Authority
One True Source

All Scripture is inspired by God and is profitable for teaching, for rebuking, for correcting, for training in righteousness...
—2 TIMOTHY 3:16

WEEK 10
The 5 & 5 Principle
In Prayer

Don't worry about anything, but in everything, through prayer and petition with thanksgiving, let your requests be made known to God.
—PHILIPPIANS 4:6

WEEK 7
Salvation
A Daily Process

For if, while we were enemies, we were reconciled to God through the death of His Son, then how much more, having been reconciled, will we be saved by His life! **—ROMANS 5:10**

WEEK 8
Authority
Three Inadequate Sources

But the unbeliever does not welcome what comes from God's Spirit, because it is foolishness to him; he is not able to understand it since it is evaluated spiritually. **—1 CORINTHIANS 2:14**